To Carrie Armento,

We enjoyed having you
on our trip to Israel. Hope
this book deepens your understanding!

In Christ

Bryant Wright

"Bryant's approach to this complicated and often explosive issue is both biblical and rational. *Seeds of Turmoil* is filled with scriptural admonitions for everyday life. You will be doubly blessed by reading it."

—Michael Youssef, PhD
Founder and president, Leading the Way,
and founding pastor of The Church of the Apostles, Atlanta, GA

"If there has ever appeared to be an insoluble situation from the human standpoint, it is the ongoing centuries-old crisis in the Middle East. As one late statesman poignantly observed, some players in this drama 'never miss an opportunity to miss an opportunity.' Unlike many of the people addressing the subject today, Bryant Wright brings a spotlight on the roots of the conflict and not simply the fruit of it. Since Scripture reveals that Jerusalem plays such a major role in the last days, every believer should have an interest and the knowledge of the *Seeds of Turmoil*. Read it and reap!"

—O. S. Hawkins
President and CEO, GuideStone Financial Resources

"My friend Bryant Wright has written an extremely interesting and thought-provoking book on one of the greatest and most difficult problems of our time and any time—the Middle East. From a historical, theological, and eschatological perspective, you will find a very balanced, fair, and yet to-the-point approach to this volatile section of the world. For those who want to learn about the Middle East conflict from a past, present, and future perspective, this book is a must-read."

—James Merritt
Senior pastor, Cross Pointe Church, Duluth, GA

"Having traveled to the Middle East with Bryant and his wife, I have witnessed the passion he has for the land and the love he has for the people. Additionally, his diligent study of both history and God's Word makes this a must-read for anyone seeking to understand a current world conflict by understanding the past. One truth comes through loud and clear: no matter how things appear, God is sovereign!"

—Eleanor Lewis
Teacher, *The Amazing Collection: The Bible Book by Book*

PRAISE FOR *SEEDS OF TURMOIL*

"In *Seeds of Turmoil* my friend Bryant Wright takes a long look back to Abraham, carefully uncovering a decision Abraham made at a critical time in his life and how it formed the basis for today's Middle East conflict."

—Andy Stanley
Senior pastor, North Point Community Church, Atlanta, GA,
and author of *The Grace of God*

"As one who has sat under Bryant Wright's preaching for several years, I have appreciated his desire to relate biblical teaching to our contemporary situation and its historical roots. *Seeds of Turmoil* follows that pattern, analyzing the current Arab-Israeli conflict against the backdrop of the history of the Middle East and its roots in the events of the Old Testament. Bryant helps us to see that, despite appearances, the world is not spinning crazily out of control but is slowly realizing God's plan for the nations. It is a gripping saga which continues to unfold before our very eyes."

—William Lane Craig, PhD
Research professor of philosophy, Talbot School of Theology,
and author of *God Is Great, God Is Good*

"Bryant Wright has provided what so many of us have needed for so long: a guide to an understanding of the Middle East conflict from a biblical rather than political perspective. It is clear, concise, scholarly, and inspired."

—Alton Brow
Food Network star, author, speaker, and host of "Good Ea

"In these days of insecurity and crises that are often centered around Middle East, *Seeds of Turmoil* helps us deal with the many quandaries questions that arise as we sort through each day's current events. Brya clarity in teaching God's Word, reflected through history and happen of this present age, opens our eyes to Truth and gives deeper insigl to the biblical meaning and origin of the problems. In spite of war political conflicts that fill news headlines, his writings enlighten us to understand God's sovereign purposes and plans."

—Larry
World Golf Hall of Famer and winner of three major PGA champ

"Bryant Wright takes one of the most compelling issues of our times and with biblical authority and clarity delivers answers to our questions regarding the Middle East—its past, present, and future. Read this book and discover the causes and God's solutions to the world's most ancient and pertinent conflict."

—Jack Graham
Senior pastor, Prestonwood Baptist Church, Plano, TX

"No matter how much we wish the coming turmoil was not coming, it is. Bryant Wright lays out a clear, biblical approach to understanding it in light of Scripture. A must-read for today's informed Christian."

—John R. Lincoln
Pastor, Shandon Baptist Church, Columbia, SC

"If you take the Bible seriously, are interested in history and current events, and are even remotely aware of the crisis at hand in the Middle East, then *Seeds of Turmoil* is a must-read. Clear, insightful, and interesting. Bryant has done us all a great favor."

—Randy Pope
Pastor, Perimeter Church, Duluth, GA

"As a communicator, Bryant Wright has a gift for making things crystal clear. As I read *Seeds of Turmoil*, I understood the Middle East conflict like never before, but what's weird is that I left the book with a real peace about it all."

—Regi Campbell
Author, *Mentor Like Jesus* and *About My Father's Business*

"This book will enable any reader to get a keen insight into the most pivotal spot in the world and history, how it got there, and where it's going. One of the finest and fairest studies on the biblical roots of the Middle East conflict I've ever read."

—Jim Henry
Former president, Southern Baptist Convention

"Bryant Wright gives great insight into the inevitable Middle East crisis, effectively building a bridge from past to present. Bryant helps to make sense of a very complex and growing issue in our global community."

—David Uth
Senior pastor, First Baptist Church, Orlando, FL

"In *Seeds of Turmoil* my friend Bryant Wright does a masterful job laying the biblical foundation for the past, present, and future turmoil in the Middle East. This is a timely and insightful book that I recommend for every pastor, leader, and student of the Bible and current events."

—Dr. Ed Young
Senior pastor, Second Baptist Church, Houston, TX

"The most important theologian in America is any pastor of a local church, and Bryant Wright shows us why. Taking the Bible in one hand and today's news in the other, Pastor Wright connects the dots with clarity, insight, and power."

—Dr. Chuck Kelley
President, New Orleans Baptist Theological Seminary

SEEDS OF
TURMOIL

SEEDS OF TURMOIL

The Biblical Roots of the Inevitable Crisis in the Middle East

BRYANT WRIGHT

THOMAS NELSON
Since 1798

NASHVILLE   DALLAS   MEXICO CITY   RIO DE JANEIRO

Published in Nashville, Tennessee, by Thomas Nelson. Thomas Nelson is a registered trademark of Thomas Nelson, Inc.

Thomas Nelson, Inc. titles may be purchased in bulk for educational, business, fund-raising, or sales promotional use. For information, please e-mail SpecialMarkets@ThomasNelson.com.

Unless otherwise noted, Scripture quotations are taken from the New American Standard Bible®, © The Lockman Foundation 1960, 1962, 1963, 1968, 1971, 1972, 1973, 1975, 1977, 1995. Used by permission.

The Scripture quotation taken from the King James Version is public domain.
Genesis 15 and Numbers 34 maps (chapter 2), illustrated by Jonathan Rhoades. Used by permission.
"City of Jerusalem" photograph (chapter 11), created by Paul and Donna Hearn. Used by permission.
Israel's Story in Maps © 2002–2010 Koret Communications (www.koret.com). All rights reserved.

Library of Congress Cataloging-in-Publication Data

Wright, Bryant.
  Seeds of turmoil : the biblical roots of the inevitable crisis in the Middle East / Bryant Wright.
    p. cm.
  Includes bibliographical references.
  ISBN 978-0-8499-4815-2 (hardcover)
  1. Abrahamic religions. 2. Bible. O.T. Genesis--Criticism, interpretation, etc. 3. Abraham (Biblical patriarch) 4. Sarah (Biblical matriarch) 5. Hagar (Biblical figure) I. Title.
  BR127.W75 2010
  222'.110830362095694—dc22

                    2010009350

Printed in the United States of America

10 11 12 13 14 QG 9 8 7 6 5 4 3 2

To Mati, whose love for the land of Israel
fueled my passion for this book

CONTENTS

ACKNOWLEDGMENTS

Writing this book has been pure joy, but bringing a book to completion is a team effort. There are so many I need to thank:

Olivia Mahon, my executive assistant, who spent countless hours typing and assisting me with research. Without her help, this book would not have been completed. The lady goes the extra mile par excellence.

Danette Ramsey, who assisted with hours of typing and research.

John Herring, who read the manuscript and assisted with the study guide.

Walt Kaiser, Archie England, Jeff Audirsch, and Wink Thompson, who were a great help with scholarly advice on this important topic.

My son, David Wright, who helped with the research.

Jonathan Rhoades and Reuven Koret, who provided the maps.

Ken Tanner, who helped me organize the original ideas for the book.

John Farish, Bob and Irene Sheridan, Pat and Alice Ann Battle, Brett and Trisha Stewart: you know the role you played.

The great folks at Thomas Nelson: Jack Countryman, who reached out to me with the idea of writing a book on a topic I'm passionate about. Thanks to my editor, Debbie Wickwire. You were great to work with. What a great coach! Matt Baugher, Jennifer Stair, Kate Etue, Paula Major, Walter Petrie, Mandi Cofer, and Rhonda Hogan—thanks to you all!

The great folks at Johnson Ferry, who have allowed me to be their pastor for so many years. Through messages and Bible studies on this topic, the groundwork was laid for this book.

My wife, Anne, who read each chapter over and over with helpful insight. She is always my greatest encourager.

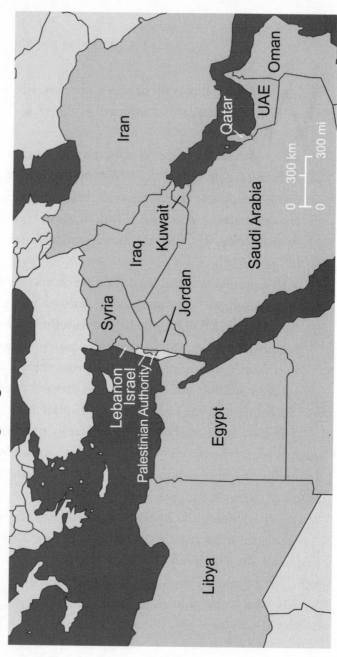

Israel and the Surrounding Region

THE BIBLICAL ROOTS
OF THE MIDDLE EAST CONFLICT

As a pastor, I'm often asked, "Bryant, why can't those people in the Middle East get along? They are always fighting about something." As I've preached on this subject, I've been surprised to learn that most people think the conflict began in 1948, when Israel became an officially recognized nation again. Even people in the church who have studied the Bible tend to think that.

No doubt 1948 was a flashpoint that inflamed hostility in the region. Immediately after Israel was declared a nation on May 14, 1948, Arab leadership from the surrounding nations told Palestinian Arabs to flee (which many did), for they planned to drive the Jews into the sea. In the 1948 Arab-Israeli War, Israel's Jews were outnumbered by the surrounding Arab nations six hundred thousand to 40 million. Their weapons were primitive. The situation from a human perspective looked hopeless. Yet miraculously, Israel survived.

However, that was not the beginning of the Middle East conflict. It goes back thousands of years—long before the Muslims conquered Jerusalem (AD 638) and long before the Romans destroyed Jerusalem and leveled the temple in AD 70, eventually expelling the Jews from their own land and renaming it Palestine. The conflict goes all the way back to Abraham, the man through whom God promised to build a great nation of His chosen people.

The only way to understand the inevitable crisis in the Middle East is to go all the way back to Abraham, the father of three very influential faiths: Judaism, Christianity, and Islam.

Abraham is honored and even revered by many as a man of great faith. Yet as faithful as he was, Abraham was guilty of a huge mistake in not trusting God at a key moment in his life. At the time, it seemed like no big deal. Yet we see the consequences of Abraham's sin almost daily in the Middle East. That's what this book is about.

Abraham is where the seeds of turmoil began.

PART ONE

THE FOUNDERS
OF THE CONFLICT

1

ONE MAN'S DECISION
Abraham

Now Sarai, Abram's wife had borne him no children,
and she had an Egyptian maid whose name was Hagar.
—GENESIS 16:1

Could a single decision, made by one person, alter the history of the world forever? It seems unlikely given the number of decisions we make each day, but consider how different your life would be if you had made other choices. Author and speaker Zig Ziglar tells of sitting on an airplane by a man whose wedding band was on the wrong hand. Ziglar recalls saying to the man, "'Friend, I can't help but notice that you've got your wedding band on the wrong finger.' [The man] smiled and replied, 'Yeah, I married the wrong woman.'"[1] What if you had married a different person—or not at all? What if you had taken another job or gone to a different school? How would your life be different?

History buffs enjoy playing a game called "alternative history." Entire books have been written to explore such questions such as, What if the

British had won the Revolutionary War?, or What if the Confederates had been victorious in the Battle of Gettysburg? One of my favorite questions in this what-if game is this: What if the Muslims had won at Tours in AD 732?

On October 10, 732, in Tours, France, after Muslims had already conquered Spain, eighty thousand Muslim cavalrymen attacked thirty thousand Frankish infantry. If they had won, there is a very good chance that Europe would have become overwhelmingly Muslim—which means North America and the United States would have as well. We would have grown up worshipping in mosques rather than in churches. That will get you thinking in light of contemporary struggles with Islam in this day and age.[2] Playing this game, we begin to see how one seemingly small event could domino into hundreds of subsequent events, eventually changing human history dramatically.

Theologians also dabble in this form of speculation with what is called "middle knowledge."[3] Since God knows all, He knows how events would have unfolded if man had made different choices along the way. It provides a background of God's sovereignty. In spite of man's bad decisions, God is still in charge. I am tempted to play this game of alternative histories and middle knowledge when I look at the ongoing conflict in the Middle East, for one man made one bad decision—and the history of that region has reaped the seeds of turmoil ever since.

The man's name was Abraham. He is revered as the father of the three most influential faiths of the world: Judaism, Christianity, and Islam. A few years ago, *Time* magazine ran a cover story entitled "The Legacy of Abraham: Muslims, Christians and Jews All Claim Him as Their Father." The reporter tells of riding in a New York City cab with the driver listening to a Moroccan group on the radio. The cabdriver asked the reporter if he wanted to know what they were singing. When the reporter said yes, the driver translated, "We have the same father; why do you treat us this way?" It was a song about Abraham called "Ishmael and Isaac."[4]

We have the same father; why do you treat us this way? This question captures the heart of the conflict that goes back about four thousand years to a story found in the book of Genesis.

GOD'S PROMISE

It had been eleven years since God had called Abraham[5] to leave his native land of Ur (in modern-day Iraq) to go to an unfamiliar land then known as Canaan, a small portion of which is now known as the state of Israel. God had promised that from Abraham and Sarah, He would make a great nation:

> Now the LORD said to Abram,
>   "Go forth from your country,
>   And from your relatives
>   And from your father's house,
>   To the land which I will show you;
>   And I will make you a great nation,
>   And I will bless you,
>   And make your name great;
>   And so you shall be a blessing;
>   And I will bless those who bless you,
>   And the one who curses you I will curse.
>   And in you all the families of the earth will be blessed."
> (Genesis 12:1–3)

And the promise got even better—God said that Abraham's heirs would inherit this magnificent land: "Abram passed through the land as far as the site of Shechem, to the oak of Moreh. Now the Canaanite was then in the land. The LORD appeared to Abram and said, 'To your descendants I will give this land.' So he built an altar there to the LORD who had appeared to him" (Genesis 12:6–7).

More than a decade after receiving this promise from God, Abraham was getting discouraged because by this time he was eighty-six years old. To make matters more complicated, his wife, Sarah, was seventy-six. Yet central to the fulfillment of God's promise of a "great nation" was having a child. No child, no great nation from the seed of Abraham. So perhaps it is understandable that Abraham was having some doubts about God's promise.

Waiting on God and His perfect timing is never easy. Perhaps you know a Christian woman who wants to get married and have children but is about to hit the big "3-0." Her biological clock is ticking rapidly. The guy she is dating is a good guy. She likes him. But love? She's not sure. She is worried about his spiritual life. She wants to marry a committed Christian man, but he simply responds, "My belief about God is a personal, private thing." She feels she's running out of time. She wonders if by marrying this guy she'll help him become a committed Christian. She's tired of waiting, and this seems to be the only guy on the horizon. Will she settle for second best or wait on God's best?

Waiting on God's best is never easy. This was Abraham and Sarah's dilemma.

ABRAHAM'S DECISION

How could God fulfill His promise to bring about a great nation through Abraham and Sarah when they were both well beyond their childbearing years? Humanly speaking, it was impossible. God saw Abraham's discouragement and was moved to encourage him. Look at the wonderful words God used to relieve those doubts: "And [God] took him outside and said, 'Now look toward the heavens, and count the stars, if you are able to count them.' And He said to him, 'So shall your descendants be'" (Genesis 15:5).

Certainly those words directly from God should have been sufficient to secure Abraham's trust and make him relax a bit. And perhaps they were for a little while. But doubt returned and, as often happens when struggling with doubts, temptation jumped directly into Abraham's path. Genesis 16:1–2 describes what happened next: "Now Sarai, Abram's wife had borne him no children, and she had an Egyptian maid whose name was Hagar. So Sarai said to Abram, 'Now behold, the LORD has prevented me from bearing children. Please go in to my maid; perhaps I will obtain children through her.' And Abram listened to the voice of Sarai."

Abraham's wife, Sarah, came up with an idea to help God out by means of a socially accepted process of having children in that ancient culture. She would have Abraham sleep with her Egyptian maid, Hagar, and their child would be the legal heir through which God would build a "great nation." It made perfect sense. Sarah would help God, blind to the fact that it meant not trusting Him.

Let's pause for a moment to understand the cultural customs of the time. Certainly if a wife made such a suggestion today, it would not be accepted by society (and probably not by the maid either). But in those days, such an act was considered permissible.[6] In fact, childless couples in the ancient Middle East had four legal options for having children: they could adopt, the husband could have a child with a second wife, the husband could have a child with a concubine, or the wife could offer her servant to her husband as a type of surrogate mother. You may think surrogate moms are a new idea for our contemporary age with artificial insemination and in vitro fertilization. Don't kid yourself. Our scientific methods may be new, but surrogacy is as old as Abraham.

All of this was culturally accepted and legal in those days. However, just because the ancient custom was legal for Abraham and Sarah did not make it right. God did not approve of this arrangement. God never intended for marriage to be polygamous. He intended for marriage to be between one man and one woman for life (Genesis 2:24). But not only that, God had promised Abraham that He would build a great nation through him *and Sarah*. He promised to give *them* a covenant child. Sarah's idea for Abraham to sleep with Hagar was, quite simply, contrary to the will of God. She was not trusting God but instead was urging Abraham to take matters into his own hands.

I imagine that Abraham wanted to please his wife. He wanted to help God out. And no doubt he liked the idea of sleeping with that young honey with his wife's encouragement.

So when Sarah came to him with this game plan, Abraham probably said something along the lines of, "Okay, whatever will make you happy. Perhaps this will help God fulfill His plan. You have a good idea. Count me in."

Abraham slept with Hagar, and she conceived.

And the problems began immediately—problems that continue to this day. Oh, to see what God's "middle knowledge" would reveal about the Middle East today had Abraham not given in to this temptation!

HISTORY IS ALTERED

Up to this point, Hagar had been Sarah's devoted servant, but now she was filled with pride. Hagar immediately changed her attitude toward her mistress, Sarah. "When [Hagar] saw that she had conceived, her mistress was despised in her sight" (Genesis 16:4). Perhaps it was just in the smug smile that she had when she looked at Sarah. Maybe she placed her hands on her stomach to subtly point out that she was carrying Abraham's child while Sarah could not. Maybe she said some cruel or harsh things to Sarah. Whatever the case, she began to be puffed up, and great tension rose between these two women. How did Sarah respond? "And Sarai said to Abram, 'May the wrong done me be upon you. I gave my maid into your arms, but when she saw that she had conceived, I was despised in her sight. May the LORD judge between you and me'" (Genesis 16:5).

Sarah was unhappy every time she saw Hagar. The baby growing in Hagar's womb represented everything that had caused sadness in Sarah's life. Sarah had blamed God for her barrenness when she tempted Abraham by saying, "The LORD has prevented me from bearing children" (Genesis 16:2). Nothing was more shameful for a wife in those days than to be barren, and Sarah was filled with resentment and a sense of failure. This says a lot about her unhappiness and the anger she had. She was also understandably outraged that her servant had turned on her. So whom did she get mad at? Abraham, of course! She blamed Abraham for an idea she thought up. Abraham was in the doghouse, big-time.

Just as many husbands today, Abraham apparently did not understand women. He had not learned that sometimes wives say things they don't really mean. And after husbands do what they think will make their wives happy, they are not. Maybe this is why the father of psychoanalysis, Sigmund Freud, wrote, "The Great Question . . . which I have not been able to answer, despite my thirty years of research into the feminine soul, is 'what does a woman want?'"[7]

We husbands are often clueless in this area. So Abraham, being a man, was likely confused about the whole thing. He just couldn't understand why Sarah was blaming him for an idea that she had. Can't you just see Abe pulling a Seinfeld—throwing up his hands and saying, "Whatever! Do whatever you want to do. I can't believe you're blaming me."

With Sarah still furious at Hagar, a catfight resulted. Hagar was carrying the baby Sarah wanted, so Sarah made life miserable for her pregnant servant. Hagar fled into the desert in complete despair and headed south, perhaps on her way back home to Egypt (Genesis 16:6). She began this walk in the desert, a dangerous if not impossible journey, especially for a pregnant woman.

Then the angel of the Lord appeared to her (Genesis 16:7). Many biblical scholars believe the angel was a theophany, a preincarnate appearance of Jesus Christ. Don't think that Christ began with His birth in Bethlehem. He always is, was, and will be.

Here we see the mercy, the compassion, and the comfort of God toward this poor slave woman who has been victimized. Because after all, Sarah was the temptress, Abraham was the sinner, and Hagar was definitely the victim in this situation. Sarah and Abraham were her masters; she had no choice but to submit to their will.

And so the angel of the Lord came to Hagar, reminding us of His love and compassion. Though Sarah's plan was not God's will, God was incredibly merciful to Hagar as He is to all who are victimized by those in power. He asked her, "Where have you come from and where are you going?" (Genesis 16:8). Hagar replied, "I am fleeing from the presence of my mistress Sarai." Then the Lord gave her a command. "Then the angel of the LORD said to her, 'Return to your mistress, and submit yourself to her authority'" (v. 9). This is not what she wanted to hear, but Hagar had to know it was the only way she and her unborn child could survive.

If you have ever seen the desert region where she was, you would wonder how anyone could ever survive more than a few days. But this was the compassion of God. Hagar needed Sarah. She needed Abraham. She had to return if she wanted to live.

Then the angel prophesied, "Look. God is going to show you mercy. A multitude of heirs will be your descendants—too many to count. And not only that, you're going to give birth to a son. You shall name him 'Ishmael' because I, God, have heard your prayer in a time of great desperation and need" (Genesis 16:10–11; author's paraphrase).

The prophecy continued. While the King James Version says, "He will be a wild man" (and I like that translation), a more literal rendering of the Hebrew would be, "He will be a wild donkey of a man" (v. 12). In other words, he will be a free and roving spirit, like a wild ass in the desert. That was not criticism; it was just a description of the untamable character Ishmael would become. And not only that, but the rest of Genesis 16:12 says,

> *His hand will be against everyone,*
> *And everyone's hand will be against him;*
> *And he will live to the east of all of his brothers.*

Once again, we should look at the original Hebrew. The actual Hebrew means, "He will live in *defiance* of his brothers." These words have great significance as we follow the actions of Ishmael's descendants.

Hagar went back, and I imagine she shared her remarkable story with Abraham and Sarah. Abraham and Hagar both obeyed the word of the Lord and named their son Ishmael.

Why is this important to you? Why is this important to the Middle East? Why is this important to the world today? Don't miss this. You need to understand what happened if you are going to understand the world in which we live today.

GOD'S PROMISE FULFILLED

God came to Abraham about fourteen years later. He was then ninety-nine years old. Abraham and Sarah still had not had a child, and Hagar's son, Ishmael, was thirteen years old. God reiterated the promise He had made to Abraham years before: He would build a great nation through Abraham's seed. Through his heir. Through his *covenant* child. God said to Abraham, "I will bless [Sarah], and indeed I will give you a son by her. Then I will bless her, and she shall be a mother of nations; kings of peoples will come from her" (Genesis 17:16).

How did Abraham respond to God's promise? He "fell on his face and laughed, and said in his heart, 'Will a child be born to a man one hundred years old? And will Sarah, who is ninety years old, bear a child?'" (v. 17).

Abraham was a rational kind of guy, and this was an honest reaction. But he also showed a serious lack of faith. He laughed before God. This was not good. Likewise, for us, it is never a good decision to laugh mockingly at the trustworthiness of God's promises in His Word. But God was patient with Abraham, as Abraham went on to say, "Oh that Ishmael might live before You!" (v. 18). It was as if Abe was saying to God, "Surely God, you must be talking about Ishmael. My teenage son. My only son. Surely you're talking about Ishmael, God." But God said, "No, but Sarah your wife will bear you a son, and you shall call his name Isaac; and I will establish My covenant with him for an everlasting covenant for his descendants after him" (v. 19).

In other words, God's plans were still in place.

GOD'S PROPHECY
CONCERNING ISHMAEL

God continued, "As for Ishmael, I have heard you; behold I will bless him, and will make him fruitful and will multiply him exceedingly. He shall become the father of twelve princes, and I will make him a great nation. But My covenant I will establish with Isaac, whom Sarah will bear to you at this season next year" (Genesis 17:20–21). God made it clear that He was still going to fulfill His plan and promise by blessing Abraham and Sarah with a son. And He made it clear that because of His grace, He was going to bless Ishmael, even though Ishmael was not the covenant child.

In Genesis 25:12–18, we see the fulfillment of God's promise and something interesting, more insight about the heirs of Ishmael: "These are the years of the life of Ishmael, one hundred and thirty-seven years; and he breathed his last and died, and was gathered to his people. They settled from Havilah to Shur which is east of Egypt as one goes toward Assyria; he settled in defiance of all his relatives" (vv. 17–18). The descendants of Ishmael settled from Havilah (modern-day Arabia) to Shur, which is east of Egypt as one goes toward Assyria (northern Iraq).[8]

Ishmael's heirs settled in this region "in defiance of all his relatives." What is that region? It's the Arabian Peninsula. It includes Saudi Arabia, Yemen, Oman, Kuwait, Qatar, United Arab Emirates, parts of Jordan and Syria, as well as southwestern Iraq below the valley area of the Tigris and Euphrates Rivers.[9] Ishmael's heirs seem to be concentrated in central and northern Arabia.[10] Wild men. Untamable. "His hand will be against everyone, / And everyone's hand will be against him" (Genesis 16:12). The prophecy of God.

But that's not all. It's interesting that the first-century historian Josephus was one of the first men to call the descendants of Ishmael "Arabs."[11] Why? Because they mostly resided in the Arabian Peninsula.

THE ROOTS OF ISLAM

Fast-forward hundreds and hundreds of years until AD 570 in what is today Saudi Arabia, when there was born a descendant of Ishmael, an Arab boy named Muhammad.

When Muhammad was forty years old, he claimed to have had a vision of God. He called on his Arab brethren to move from polytheism to monotheism, worshipping one god called Allah. Here is something that may surprise you. Originally, Muhammad did not consider himself as having started a new religion. Instead, he saw his role as bringing about a completion or purification of the Old Testament and the New Testament, of Judaism and Christianity. But when the Jews and Christians rejected his false teachings, Muhammad turned against them.

Islam is the perfect false teaching to be embraced by the Arab people to fulfill the prophecy God made to Hagar. Remember, God told Hagar that "her son would be a wild donkey of a man," a wild man in the desert, residing in the Arabian Peninsula, and his hand would be against others and everyone's hand would be against him. Not only does the Qur'an command Muslims to "slay the infidel" (Sura 9:5), but even among Muslims themselves there is great hostility to this day (think of the conflict between Shiites and Sunnis, which will be explained in chapter 10).

Is the light starting to come on? Had Abraham waited on God, trusted God, and obeyed the will of God, there would not have been an Ishmael or the deep-rooted turmoil we see in the Middle East today. It all goes back to a single decision by one man. It probably didn't seem like a big deal at the time; Abraham was just following the accepted customs of the day. But his decision to sleep with Hagar was, in fact, sin—not trusting God—and sin always has negative consequences.

Yes, God is compassionate. He is merciful. We see that in His actions toward Hagar and Ishmael. And we see God's faithfulness when He keeps His promise to Abraham and Sarah. But God doesn't remove the negative consequences of our sin. Almost every day, the news from the Middle East reminds us of Abraham's sin—and how long-term the negative consequences of sin can be.

2

AN EVERLASTING POSSESSION
The Holy Land

The LORD appeared to Abram and said, "To your descendants I will give this land." So he built an altar there to the LORD who had appeared to him.

—GENESIS 12:7

We've explored how the Middle East conflict goes back to one man's decision, but why all of this controversy over the land? Today's news constantly reminds us of the dispute over who has rights to the area commonly referred to as "the Holy Land." The hottest disputes are over the West Bank, the Golan Heights, the Gaza Strip, and the Muslim and Jewish Quarters in Jerusalem. So what is it about the land that is central to the conflict?

Central to the Holy Land is the nation of Israel—as shown in this map, a small area about the size of New Jersey, home to nearly 6 million Jews who are surrounded by approximately 400 million Arab Muslims. The first question might be, if this is the land of

Washington DC

© 2003 Koret Communications Ltd. www.koret.com

Israel/US size comparison

their forefathers, aren't the Jews entitled to it? Remember, God clearly promised this land to Abraham's heirs: "To your descendants I will give this land" (Genesis 12:7).

A quick historical overview will help us better understand the situation today.

THE ORIGIN OF PALESTINE

"Of all the writings held sacred by the world's religions, only the Bible presents a message linked to geography."[1] I'm sure this is why I feel so at home every time I visit the Holy Land. Nothing looks the same as Atlanta. But everywhere we go, we see geographical sites described in Scripture. The Jews began to claim the land under Joshua, the successor to Moses, more than four hundred years after Abraham. The book of Joshua describes this process that occurred from about 1250 to 1200 BC. Later, around 1000 BC, under King David, Israel conquered the Jebusites and claimed Jerusalem as the capital of Israel. This is described in 2 Samuel 5:6–10.

In AD 70, the Roman Empire grew tired of the Jews' resentment and revolts against Roman rule and sacked Jerusalem. Jews began to be dispersed from their homeland by the Romans. In a final revolt in AD 135, all Jews were completely expelled from Israel.

To add insult to injury, the Romans chose the name Palestine, a Roman derivative of the word *Philistine*, the longtime enemies of ancient Israel whose stronghold was in Gaza (now referred to as the Gaza Strip) and used it to rename the land of Israel. Interestingly, you won't find the word *Palestine* in the Bible because it did not exist. You might think you've seen it, but it's not in the text, only on some of the man-made maps. Since *Palestine* is a Roman derivative of *Philistine*, Yasser Arafat and the Palestine Liberation Organization (PLO) movement claimed to be modern-day heirs of the Philistines and thus hold a claim to the land long before the Jews. Legitimate historians see that as dubious at best. But more about Arafat and the PLO later.

With this being such an arid, desertlike region, you may wonder why

Rome would even want this land. They wanted it for the same reasons every great ancient empire wanted it: transportation. It was the primary corridor for the trade route between three major continents: Africa, Asia, and Europe, a sacred bridge, if you will—a land bridge.[2] If a person in the ancient world wanted to travel from Africa to Europe or Asia, they would go along the Mediterranean Sea—east to Asia and northwest to Europe. Palestine was the crossroads of the world.

MUSLIM DOMINATION OF THE LAND

The western portion of the Roman Empire, headquartered in Rome, fell in AD 476. The eastern portion, headquartered in Constantinople (now Istanbul, Turkey), lasted another one thousand years until 1453. After the fall of the western portion of Rome's empire, the land known as Palestine became largely a wasteland, although Jerusalem held fascination because of its religious and historical interest. Out of this leaderless vacuum came the Muslim conquest in AD 638.

Like Christianity in the first century, Islam spread through the Middle East and North Africa like a raging fire. Yet unlike Christianity, which preaches conversion through the gospel of Christ received through faith, Islam believes in conversion by conquest, by power—including military power. Islam means "submission"—submission to Allah. And people under Muslim rule are expected to submit. If necessary, this comes by coercion or force. Muslim Arabs and Muslim Turks ruled the region until World War I, when Ottoman Turks surrendered control of Palestine to the British. We'll discuss this more later.

THE ZIONIST MOVEMENT

Beginning in the 1880s, some Jewish intellectuals living in Europe, realizing they would always face anti-Semitism and discrimination in Europe and

Russia, began to call for their own land—a national homeland for the Jews. In 1894, a Jewish French army officer by the name of Captain Alfred Dreyfus was accused of selling secrets to Germany. The evidence was nonexistent, but he was court-martialed to life in prison on Devil's Island in French Guiana. Many Frenchmen simply believed a Jew could not be a loyal Frenchman.

Watching all this was an Austrian Jewish journalist by the name of Theodor Herzl. He became convinced that the Jews would never find a home in non-Jewish societies. As a result, he became the visionary for what is called the Zionist Movement, the call for a Jewish homeland in the land of their ancient forefathers in what was called Palestine. Herzl was more motivated by his Jewish ethnic identity and economic opportunity than religion. For many Jewish intellectuals in Europe, religion was more like a tradition—a part of ethnic heritage—than a personal reality. In that regard, Herzl was like many Jews in America today in the Reformed, and in some cases, the Conservative branches of American Judaism.

Herzl and his growing Zionist Movement felt that the Hebrew language needed to be revived beyond the use by Jewish rabbis and memorization for bar mitzvahs. He believed Jewish culture should be taught with the hopes that a Jewish nation could be founded. (By the way, *Zion* is the poetic Hebrew name for the Holy Land.)

Herzl organized the first Zionist Congress in Basel, Switzerland, in 1897. As the movement grew, some courageous Jewish pioneers settled in the land of Palestine when there wasn't much there in terms of natural resources and population. But Jewish Zionists felt there would never be security for the Jewish people until they had their own land, their own nation. Remember, Zionism is more about the land than the Jewish religion. The religion, and its tradition, is just one component.

THE BRITS AND THE BALFOUR DECLARATION

After World War I, with Great Britain in charge of Palestine, Arthur James Balfour issued the Balfour Declaration of 1917. It reads in part: "His

Majesty's government view with favour the establishment in Palestine of a national home for the Jewish people, and will use their best endeavors to facilitate the achievement of this object, it being clearly understood that nothing shall be done which may prejudice the civil and religious rights of existing non-Jewish communities in Palestine, or the rights and political status enjoyed by Jews in any other country."[3] What is interesting is, "Balfour's keen interest in Zionism was prepared at least in part by his Sunday school faith, a case put forth by Balfour's biographer and niece, Blanch Dugdale."[4] In 1914, Balfour told the leading Jewish Zionist of his day (Chaim Weizmann) that in his view, the Jewish situation "would remain insoluble until either the Jews here became entirely assimilated or there was a normal Jewish community in Palestine."[5]

One thing is for sure: in 1917, Britain's culture had a much stronger biblical Christian influence than could be imagined in secular Britain today. This declaration appealed to justice for the Jews based on their biblical heritage. Balfour served in the cabinet of British prime minister David Lloyd George, who was a Bible-believing Christian.

British historian Paul Johnson wrote, "Lloyd George was a Bible-thumper, another point in Zionists' favour." He noted that when Zionist Jewish leaders talked of Palestine, Lloyd George said that they "kept bringing up place-names which were more familiar to me than those on the Western Front."[6] With the Jews expelled from their land in the late first century and early second century, the Brits came to the rescue of the "chosen people" of the Bible while attaching themselves to the growing Zionist Movement of the Jewish intelligentsia of Europe. Whatever the motive, the sovereignty of God was at work.

As you can imagine, the Arab Muslims of the Middle East were not happy; but they sought comfort in the wording of the Balfour Declaration that a Jewish homeland would never come about unless they agreed to it, something they had no intention of doing—for Islam is about submission to Allah. When they conquered the land in AD 638, it was for the glory of Allah. In their view, to give up the land would be against the will of Allah, who gave them victory in the land.

MODERN-DAY ISRAEL

Sometimes great events in history come about when two separate movements come together at the same time with a common interest. Britain's biblical Christian heritage and political interest for her empire, along with the growing Zionism of European Jews, created great momentum for European Jews moving to Palestine. This was resented by Palestinian Arabs, who felt their forefathers rightfully claimed it in 638. Yet a steady stream of Jewish pioneers began to migrate to Palestine. By the late 1800s, what had been about 20,000 Jews living in Palestine had more than doubled.[7]

By the 1930s, with the momentum of the Balfour Declaration and Zionism among European Jews, along with a growing menace out of Germany called *fascism* under Adolf Hitler, the Jewish population in Palestine grew to more than 250,000. Then on November 29, 1947, with the Western world's guilt over what Hitler's Nazi philosophy had wrought—namely, the extermination of almost 6 million Jews in the Holocaust—the United Nations passed a resolution calling for a Jewish and Arab state in a divided land of Palestine. The UN General Assembly Resolution 181 says, in part: "Independent Arab and Jewish States and the Special International Regime for the City of Jerusalem, set forth in part III of this plan, shall come into existence in Palestine two months after the evacuation of the armed forces of the mandatory Power has been completed but in any case not later than 1 October 1948. The boundaries of the Arab State, the Jewish State, and the City of Jerusalem shall be as described in parts II and III . . ."[8]

Five Arab nations (Egypt, Jordan, Lebanon, Iraq, and Syria) threatened war if the UN resolution passed. Yet on May 14, 1948, the nation of Israel was reborn and declared a state. The first nation to recognize Israel as an official state on that day was the United States under President Harry Truman. President Truman did this despite intense opposition from many in his cabinet, including General George Marshall, who was already a legend in popular opinion.[9] Truman's decision was motivated by his knowledge of scriptures such as Deuteronomy 1:8: "See, I have placed the land before you; go in and possess the land which the LORD swore to give to your fathers, to Abraham, to Isaac, and to Jacob, to them and their descendants after them."[10]

1947 UN Partition Plan

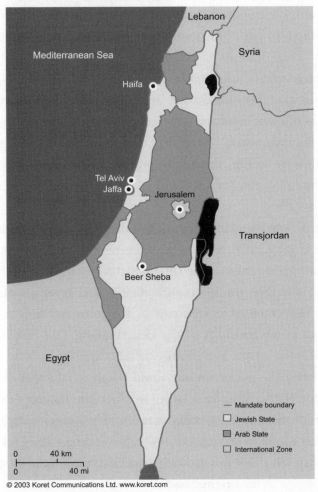

© 2003 Koret Communications Ltd. www.koret.com

THE 1948 ARAB-ISRAELI WAR

The Arab and Muslim world was appalled when Israel was officially recognized as a state. They viewed the UN resolution as an insult to Allah, who had given them the land. Arab Palestinians, who had lived in the land for more than thirteen hundred years, were outraged. The next day, good to their word, the five Arab nations declared war on Israel and told Arab Palestinians to flee, for they were going to "push the Jews into the sea."[11] Seven hundred thousand Palestinian refugees fled into these surrounding Arab nations. With practically no weapons and with only six hundred thousand Jews surrounded by tens of millions of Arab Muslims,[12] the Jews of the newly reinstated Israel looked hopeless.

It is interesting to note that in a 1947 report that is now declassified, the CIA predicted this: "Unless they are able to obtain significant outside aid in terms of manpower and material, the Jews will be able to hold out no longer than two years."[13] In spite of this prediction, just one year after these words were written, the Israelis prevailed, and a truce was declared between the Arabs and Jews. It is one of the modern miracles of history that Israel survived.

To get a better understanding, consider how an American citizen would feel if the United Nations passed a resolution declaring that the original thirteen colonies of the United States be returned to the Native Americans, with their traditions and religions and government and culture to be implemented in that part of the country. Many Americans would laugh at the absurdity of the idea, thinking, *Our forefathers took that land fair and square, and we are entitled to keep it.*

But what if the powers in our world began to take this declaration seriously and Native Americans began to move into the thirteen original colonies in droves and even staked a claim to Washington DC, as their capital? That would likely mean civil war. Now you get a feel for how the Arab Muslims felt about this growing worldwide movement to return the land of Palestine to the original owners—the Jews.

THE PALESTINIAN LIBERATION ORGANIZATION (PLO)

Since May 14, 1948, the conflict over the land in the modern state of Israel has been brutal. This intensified in the 1960s with the formation of the Palestinian Liberation Organization (PLO). In 1969, Yasser Arafat was elected chairman. The PLO's charter called for the elimination of Israel, stating, "The liberation of Palestine, from an Arab viewpoint, is a national (*qawmi*) duty and it attempts to repel the Zionist and imperialist aggression against the Arab homeland, and aims at the elimination of Zionism in Palestine."[14] Articles 19 and 20 go on to add interesting insight.

> Article 19: The partition of Palestine in 1947 and the establishment of the state of Israel are entirely illegal, regardless of the passage of time, because they were contrary to the will of the Palestinian people and to their natural right in their homeland, and inconsistent with the principles embodied in the Charter of the United Nations, particularly the right to self-determination.
>
> Article 20: The Balfour Declaration, the Mandate for Palestine, and everything that has been based upon them, are deemed null and void. Claims of historical or religious ties of Jews with Palestine are incompatible with the facts of history and the true conception of what constitutes statehood. Judaism, being a religion, is not an independent nationality. Nor do Jews constitute a single nation with an identity of its own; they are citizens of the states to which they belong.[15]

Obviously, this is a total rejection of a Jewish homeland in Palestine.

THE SIX-DAY WAR

On June 5, 1967, with Egyptian military mobilizing in the Sinai region for what appeared to be an attack on Israel, the Israelis engaged in a preemptive strike that destroyed the Egyptian and Syrian air force before it could

get off the ground. This decisive war, lasting only six days, stunned the
world. How in the world could this tiny nation the size of New Jersey have
such an incredible victory? By the end of the week, Israel claimed Gaza,
the Sinai Peninsula, the Golan Heights, the West Bank, and the Temple
Mount in Jerusalem.

June 10, 1967: Israel After the Six Day War

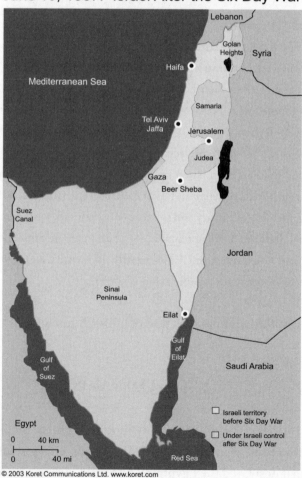

© 2003 Koret Communications Ltd. www.koret.com

Like surviving the 1948 Arab-Israeli War during the first year of her rebirth, the 1967 Six-Day War was once again a miraculous military victory of biblical proportions. The Arab world was humiliated, and even worse, they viewed the defeat as humiliation to Allah, who had given them the land. The pressure of the world led Israel to return most of the land of the Sinai Peninsula and parts of the West Bank, but to this day they refuse to return Jerusalem.

An Unconditional Covenant

This short historical journey from the demolishing of Jerusalem by Rome in AD 70 through the conquest of Jerusalem by Arab Muslims in AD 638, on to the Zionist Movement and the Balfour Declaration, and finally into the rebirth of Israel and the Six-Day War only partially explains the conflict. Though significant, this historical background of Israel actually misses what is most important. We read in Genesis 12:1–2 that God called Abraham and gave him a promise. You'll remember that Abraham's family was from Ur, in modern-day Iraq. At seventy-five years of age, he was led by God to leave his native land and on faith go to a land he did not know.

Imagine your boss coming to you and telling you, "The company needs you to make a move. We've got plans for you." It's a time in your life when you are near retirement and settled in the community.

Stunned, you respond, "Where?"

Your boss says, "I'm not going to tell you yet. Just sell your house, pack up your family and all your belongings, and start heading southwest. Keep your cell phone on, and when you get to where we want you to go, we'll call you."

"How will you know?" you reply.

"We'll keep up with your company car on satellite."

How would you respond? You'd think they were wacko.

About the time most people should have already retired, Abraham was asked to make a big move. Abraham had a huge amount of faith and amazing courage to trust God. He did what God asked him and headed southwest with his wife, some relatives, and all of his possessions. As they traveled, Abraham surely wondered about the other aspect of God's promise we've already discussed—the fact that he was seventy-five and Sarah was sixty-five, and they had been barren all of their married life. Abraham probably thought, *We are running out of time. It already seems way too late.* But he kept moving on faith.

God's Word tells us of the journey:

> So Abram went forth as the LORD had spoken to him; and Lot went with him. Now Abram was seventy-five years old when he departed from Haran. Abram took Sarai his wife and Lot his nephew, and all their possessions which they had accumulated, and the persons which they had acquired in Haran, and they set out for the land of Canaan; thus they came to the land of Canaan. Abram passed through the land as far as the site of Shechem, to the oak of Moreh. Now the Canaanite was then in the land. The LORD appeared to Abram and said, "To your descendants I will give this land." So he built an altar there to the LORD who had appeared to him. (Genesis 12:4–7)

God led Abraham to Canaan, the land of an ancient pagan people group. Then God told Abraham that He would give this land to his *heirs.* Not to Abraham. Not to Sarah. But to their heirs. Pioneers have the struggles; heirs have the benefits. What selflessness on Abraham's part.

About ten years later, when Abraham was having some doubts about God's promise of the land, God reassured him that his descendants would be given the land. "I am the LORD who brought you out of Ur of the Chaldeans, to give you this land to possess it" (Genesis 15:7). But Abraham was not so sure. He said, "O Lord GOD, how may I know that I will possess it?" (v. 8)

Then God did something Abraham would understand. In the ancient Middle East, a covenant was made when an animal was cut in two and the two parties in agreement walked between the halves to seal the deal. In

Genesis 15:9–16, Abraham brought animals to God and cut them in two, and then he went into a deep sleep. He didn't walk through the halves of the carcasses, but God did. "It came about when the sun had set, that it was very dark, and behold, there appeared a smoking oven and a flaming torch which passed between these pieces" (Genesis 15:17). It was like God sealed the covenant and was saying to Abraham, "This one's on Me." This covenant was not conditional on Abraham's faithfulness, unlike so many of the Old Testament covenants that are based on Israel's obedience ("If you do this . . . then I will . . .").

As part of this covenant, God gave Abraham the geographical boundaries:

> On that day the LORD made a covenant with Abram, saying,
>   *"To your descendants I have given this land,*
>   *From the river of Egypt as far as the great river, the river Euphrates:*
> the Kenite and the Kenizzite and the Kadmonite
> and the Hittite and the Perizzite and the Rephaim
> and the Amorite and the Canaanite and the Girgashite and
> the Jebusite." (Genesis 15:18–21)

The promised land would extend all the way back toward Abraham's homeland—all the way northeast to the Euphrates River in modern-day Syria, and all the way west to the river of Egypt. But God did not include clear north-south boundaries (although one could argue that the Euphrates River is just as much a northern border as an eastern border, with the Jordan River down to the Dead Sea serving as a clearer eastern border in the southern portion of the promised land.)[16] God simply said that Abraham's heirs would inherit the land of all the "-ites"—the Kenites and the Kenizzites and the Kadmonites and the Hittites and the Perizzites and the Rephaim and the Amorites and the Canaanites and the Girgashites and the Jebusites. Those "-ite" families were quite numerous.

Through the years, I have spoken with several Old Testament scholars about what would be the modern-day boundaries of the land God promised Abraham's heirs. On the west, the Mediterranean Sea is indisputable.

To the northeast, portions of the Euphrates River are the dominant view. How far to the east is a bit blurry. To the south, there are also different opinions, with the Nile River being the dominant view though great scholars differ on this as well. To add to the complication, the "ite" groups were nomadic. Modern scholars don't have a clear geographical area to pinpoint where they lived.

Not long ago, I took a course on Joshua under Old Testament scholar Walter Kaiser, president emeritus of Gordon-Conwell Theological Seminary and editor of the *NIV Archeological Study Bible*. He felt that the southern boundary of the promised land is at the Wadi of Egypt, sometimes called the Brook of Egypt, about twenty miles south of Gaza. It extends from the Mediterranean Sea directly to modern-day Elat at the northern tip of the Gulf of Aqaba, which is the southern border of modern-day Israel. The eastern border goes north to the Dead Sea along the Jordan River and then at some point makes a sharp right turn to encompass the Golan Heights and the region around Damascus in modern-day Syria until reaching the northern boundary, which is along the el-Kabir River at the northern border of modern-day Lebanon. My interpretation of Dr. Kaiser's view is depicted in this map:

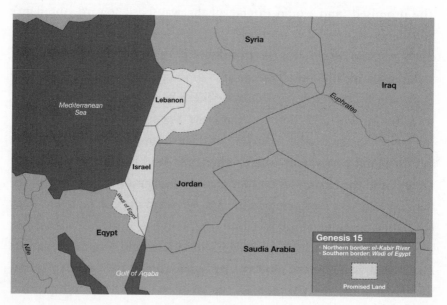

Other scholars, including the translators of the New American Standard Bible, believe that the northern boundary is along the Euphrates River. It extends east to central Syria, with a sharp southward turn toward the Golan Heights and then due south along the Jordan River and Dead Sea to Elat. Either way, the promised land would encompass the northeastern portion of Egypt, some of Jordan, some of Syria, and all of Lebanon, along with the modern-day nation of Israel. My interpretation of this view of the promised land is shown in the map below.

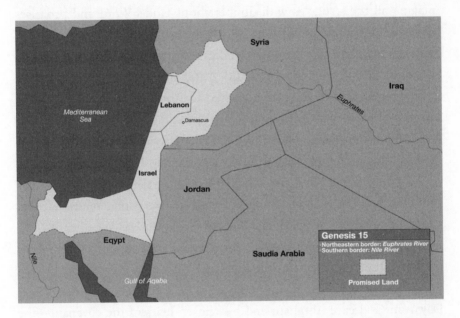

I believe this map makes the most sense in light of Scripture. Second Kings 24:7 speaks to the southern border as being the brook of Egypt: "The king of Egypt did not come out of his land again, for the king of Babylon had taken all that belonged to the king of Egypt from the brook of Egypt to the river Euphrates." Nonbiblical sources are clear that the brook of Egypt taken over by the king of Babylon was the Nile. Many biblical scholars agree. One thing is for sure. The land God promised Abraham is far greater than the land of the modern-day nation of Israel.

We think the conflict over the land in the Middle East is bad today. Can you imagine what would happen if the modern state of Israel announced to the world that they were going to claim all of the land God promised them? It would be World War III for sure.

AN EVERLASTING POSSESSION

But it gets even more interesting. Fast-forward fourteen more years after God's covenant with Abraham. Still no children. Still no land. Can you imagine all the struggles with doubts about God's Word and promises Abraham and Sarah have battled during the last twenty-four years? Yet in spite of a huge mistake thirteen years earlier in trying to help God out by having a child through Sarah's maid, Abraham still believed. As we saw in chapter 1, God once again appeared to Abraham and reiterated His promises. In Genesis 17:8, God says this about the land: "I will give to you and to your descendants after you, the land of your sojournings, all the land of Canaan, for an everlasting possession; and I will be their God."

God promised Abraham and his heirs that they would receive the promised land as an "everlasting possession." Everlasting means eternal. Everlasting means forever. Could God have been clearer? Whether 587 BC, when Nebuchadnezzar of Babylon conquered Jerusalem and took most of the Jews out of their land and into the Babylonian captivity; or AD 70, when Rome destroyed the temple in Jerusalem; or May 14, 1948; or the 1967 Six-Day War, God gave Abraham and his chosen heirs of the covenant—the Hebrew people, the nation of Israel—the land as an *everlasting possession*.

God didn't just make this promise one time. He reiterated it to Isaac (Genesis 26), to Jacob (Genesis 28), and then four hundred years later to Moses in Numbers 34. My interpretation of the land as described in this passage appears in the map on the opposite page:

Then the LORD spoke to Moses, saying, "Command the sons of Israel and say to them, 'When you enter the *land of Canaan,* this is the land that shall fall to you as an inheritance, even the land of Canaan according to its borders. Your southern sector shall extend from the wilderness of Zin along the side of Edom, and your southern border shall extend from the end of the Salt Sea eastward. Then your border shall turn direction from the south to the ascent of Akrabbim and continue to Zin, and its termination shall be to the south of Kadesh-barnea; and it shall reach Hazaraddar and continue to Azmon. The border shall turn direction from Azmon to the brook of Egypt, and its termination shall be at the sea.

As for the western border, you shall have the Great Sea, that is, its coastline; this shall be your west border.

And this shall be your north border: you shall draw your border line from the Great Sea to Mount Hor. You shall draw a line from Mount Hor to the Lebo-hamath, and the termination of the border shall be at Zedad; and the border shall proceed to Ziphron, and its termination shall be at Hazar-enan. This shall be your north border.

For your eastern border you shall also draw a line from Hazar-enan to Shepham, and the border shall go down from Shepham to Riblah on the east side of Ain; and the border shall go down and reach to the slope on the east side of the Sea of Chinnereth. And the border shall go down to the Jordan and its termination shall be at the Salt Sea. This shall be your land according to its borders all around.'" (Numbers 34:1–12; emphasis added; cf. Exodus 23:31)

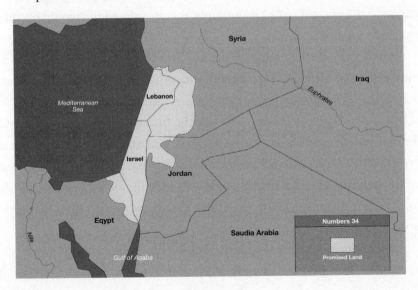

This description of the promised land is smaller than the one God gave to Abraham in Genesis 15 and reiterated as an everlasting promise in Genesis 17. I wish I could give you a concise, clear reasoning, but some things in Scripture are simply unexplainable. There are a few things to keep in mind, the first being the absolute trustworthiness of God's Word. At times, reading various passages of Scripture can seem contradictory. This can cause us to doubt the trustworthiness of God's Word. I know. I've dealt with those doubts many times. But once we have settled the issue that Scripture is perfectly true and trustworthy, then we learn to doubt our doubts and ask God, "What insight are You trying to share with me?" Sometimes we simply have to trust that God's Word is true even when it is difficult to understand. And sometimes, over time, claims of Scripture that at first seem contradictory become clear through the interpretation and teaching of the Holy Spirit. We realize there is no contradiction. We just didn't have a full understanding culturally, historically, and theologically. That may well be the case here.

Second, the description of the promised land in Numbers is consistent with other historical records of the land of Canaan. For instance, the land of Canaan was used in Egyptian literature as early as the second millennium BC. So it seems to have been a commonly accepted geographical region in the ancient world.[17] Certainly, the promised land would encompass the land of Canaan.

And finally, at this point in history, God was leading Moses to guide the children of Israel in claiming the land of Canaan. It doesn't mean that the promised land would ultimately be limited to the land of Canaan. Yet at this time in Israel's history, this was the focus God wanted Moses and the children of Israel to have. One thing is for sure: the promised land as described to Abraham and now to Moses is a much larger piece of real estate than modern-day Israel. Obviously, we will not see the final fulfillment of this promise of God until the Messiah comes and rules the world from Jerusalem.

After Moses's death, God reiterated His promise to Moses's successor, Joshua, and told him it was time to claim the land (Joshua 1:2–6). It took about fifty years, but eventually Joshua claimed much but not all of it. The nation of Israel reached its zenith in conquering the land under King David and his son Solomon. Yet the Israelites never have completely claimed or conquered all the land God promised them. And certainly today in the modern nation of Israel, much of the promise of God's Word concerning the land is yet to be realized.

AN IRRESOLVABLE CONFLICT?

God's promise to Israel doesn't solve the conflict. In many ways, it heightens the tension. Combine this with Islam's emphasis on submission to Allah and their belief that Allah gave them the land that is modern-day Israel in AD 638, and Israel's presence and existence in the land is an outrageous humiliation to Allah. Today, about 6 million Jews in Israel are surrounded by approximately 400 million Arab Muslims, and Arab Muslims still can't claim the land they feel is rightfully theirs. This is unacceptable to Allah and their religion.

Humanly speaking, this is an irresolvable dilemma. From the Muslim Arabic view, they owned the land for more than thirteen hundred years (638–1948), and outside forces (like the UN, led by the US and Great Britain) gave their land to the Jews. Humanly speaking, it is a travesty, a gross injustice. The heirs of Abraham and Ishmael feel they are getting a raw deal from the heirs of Abraham and Isaac again.

Yet if God's Word is true, the heirs of Abraham, Isaac, and Jacob— the nation of Israel—are entitled to the land. It is a promise of God as an *everlasting possession*. It's hard to see how a Bible-believing Christian could not be supportive of Israel's ownership of the land.

I've traveled to the Holy Land countless times. I wish I could go tomorrow. There is something special about it. Bible-believing Christians have a special attachment and affection for the land. It's the land of Israel and the land to which God chose to send His Son. It's the land where Jesus walked and lived. It's the land where Jesus gave His life for man's sin on a Roman cross. It's the land where He rose from the dead and conquered sin and death so that we might too. It's the land where He ascended into heaven, and it's the land where He's coming again. No words can describe how special is the promised land—the Holy Land.

Though humanly speaking the conflict over the land seems irresolvable, one day the Messiah will come again and touch down on the Mount of Olives. "In that day His feet will stand on the Mount of Olives, which is in front of Jerusalem on the east; and the Mount of Olives will be split in its middle from east to west by a very large valley, so that half of the mountain will move toward the north and the other half toward the south" (Zechariah 14:4). The Messiah will enter Jerusalem to reign as King of kings and Lord of lords. He will reign from the throne of David in Jerusalem. "And the LORD will be king over all the earth; in that day the LORD will be the only one, and His name the only one . . . Then it will come about that any who are left of all the nations that went against Jerusalem will go up from year to year to worship the King, the LORD of hosts, and to celebrate the Feast of Booths" (Zechariah 14:9, 16).

Until that time, all the peace treaties in the world will be temporary truces. For only then, when the Lord returns, will the conflict over the land in the Middle East be resolved.

3

Two Women
Who Shaped History

Sarah and Hagar

*After Abram had lived ten years in the land of Canaan, Abram's
wife Sarai took Hagar the Egyptian, her maid, and gave her to her husband
Abram as his wife. He went in to Hagar, and she conceived; and when
she saw that she had conceived, her mistress was despised in her sight.*

—Genesis 16:3–4

Through the years, I've asked thousands of people to tell me about
their spiritual lives—to tell me how they discover God's will.
Over and over I've heard the response, "Well, you know . . . God
helps those who help themselves." Occasionally I've responded, "This
may be America's favorite Bible verse, but I'm sorry to have to tell you—it
ain't in the Bible." Many look at me bewildered, disbelieving. Sometimes
they protest, "It's got to be in there. I've heard it all my life—my mama
taught me that verse."

But it's not, even though many people claim it as their favorite verse. It was actually a saying made popular by a great American who probably got impatient with Christians who would say things like, "I'm just trusting the Lord" or "It's all up to God" or "I'm just waiting on the Lord." That great American was named Ben Franklin, and even though his common-sense saying from *Poor Richard's Almanac*[1] is often believed to be biblical wisdom, it is not. As a matter of fact, this well-intentioned but misguided philosophy has caused many to take matters into their own hands in a way that shows a lack of trust in God and His promises.

But it's not just Americans who buy into the philosophy of Ben Franklin and feel they are doing right in the process. Some of the biblical giants of the faith thought and acted this way, and when they did, it shaped the course of history.

One of those was Sarah, the wife of Abraham—one of the great women in Scripture. Sarah bought into the idea "God helps those who help themselves" thousands of years before Ben Franklin wrote it down as American common sense.

A PRAGMATIC PLAN

Sarah had a big problem—barrenness (Genesis 16:1–2). Infertility is a heart-wrenching dilemma. We are reminded of this every Mother's Day. Some stay away from church on that Sunday because the pain is so great. These women are so grieved at not being able to have a child, they know they would be miserable on a day when all the focus is on motherhood.

But as painful as infertility is in our culture, it was doubly painful in ancient days. In those days, barrenness was more than a physiological issue; it was considered to be a spiritual issue. It was a sign of God's disfavor on a married woman's life. It wasn't just grief; it was shame. Sarah had dealt with this shame throughout her adult life. Then to add to her frustration, God promised her husband that He would give them a son—a promise that was physically impossible at their advanced age. At age sixty-five, Sarah was well beyond childbearing years. In modern times, the oldest woman known to have conceived naturally was fifty-nine.[2]

A decade went by—and Abraham was eighty-five. Ten years his junior, Sarah knew she was not getting any younger either. Abraham may have told her that God came to reassure him that He would keep His promise that from his seed would come more than the stars he could see in the heavens. God had told Abraham, "Now look toward the heavens, and count the stars, if you are able to count them . . . So shall your descendants be" (Genesis 15:5).

Yet Sarah was evidently having a difficult time believing God's promise to Abraham. So one day she looked at her Egyptian servant and had an idea. The servant's name was Hagar, and Sarah came up with a way to help God out. She wanted to believe God. She wanted to believe her husband—but she was a pragmatist. They had been waiting long enough—so long that she rationalized, "God helps those who help themselves." Since it was a legally accepted practice in those days for the husband of a barren wife to conceive a child with his wife's servant, Hagar fit the bill. Why didn't she think of this sooner? *Maybe*, Sarah thought, *God has been waiting on me to suggest this for a long time.*

So Sarah went to Abraham with an idea. "Now behold, the LORD has prevented me from bearing children. Please go in to my maid; perhaps I will obtain children through her" (Genesis 16:2). Sarah was saying three things to Abraham. First of all, she blamed God for her barrenness. Certainly it was God's will at this point for her not to have a child, but her barrenness wasn't punishment. It was just not God's timing. Sarah could have said, "God has prevented me from having children up to this point, but I believe the word of God that came to my husband, Abraham. One day He will give us a child and eventually build a great people through him." Yet Sarah didn't say that.

Second, Sarah came up with a way to help God out when He needed no help. She urged her husband to "go in to her maid." The Hebrew could not be more graphic in communicating that Sarah was urging her husband to have sexual intercourse with another woman. This was legal, but not God's will. This was pragmatic, but not God's plan. It was socially acceptable, but not what God wanted them to do.

Finally, Sarah made what she may have considered to be a realistic statement of faith. "Perhaps I will obtain children through her" (Genesis 16:2). Basically, she was thinking, *I don't know for sure if Hagar will become pregnant from your seed, Abraham—only God knows—but if we'll show a little faith here and give this plan I've thought up a chance, maybe God will bless it. It's worth a try.* Ben Franklin would have been proud. Think up a plan, show some initiative, and then ask God to bless your idea.

Like any good husband, Abraham wanted to please his wife. "Abram listened to the voice of Sarai" (Genesis 16: 2). Maybe she was on to something. And because Abraham was a sinner—like all of us—he probably thought, *I'd love to sleep with this other woman—especially if my wife is suggesting it.* Note there was no argument from Abraham that this was not God's plan. No argument from Abraham that this might create jealousy with Sarah if Hagar got pregnant. No argument that waiting on God can deepen and strengthen a person's faith. After all, maybe she was right.

In agreeing to Sarah's plan, Abraham was giving in to the toughest kind of temptation to sin—temptations that come through those we love, especially temptation that comes to a man through the woman he loves. We are reminded of the incredible influence a wife has on her husband for good or for bad. To trust God or not to trust. It is as old as Adam and Eve. A wife's power to influence her husband's actions is powerful indeed. Sarah influenced Abraham to sin, and she shaped the course of history in a way that is still reverberating through Middle East conflict today.

Genesis 16:4 says, "He went in to Hagar, and she conceived; and when she saw that she had conceived, her mistress was despised in her sight." Sarah's plan worked, and problems in the Middle East began. As soon as she realized she was pregnant, Hagar began to flaunt it in front of Sarah. This had not been Hagar's idea, but since Sarah had thought it up and Hagar was powerless to oppose it, she decided to make life miserable for

Sarah. Then Sarah unloaded on Abraham for going along with her idea and adding to the misery of her life. "May the wrong done me be upon you. I gave my maid into your arms, but when she saw that she had conceived, I was despised in her sight. May the LORD judge between you and me" (Genesis 16:5).

Abraham, of course, was baffled at Sarah's response and put it back on her. He said, in essence, "Look, she's your maid. You have power over her—do with her whatever you feel best." So Sarah made life so miserable for Hagar that she fled. Her pragmatism worked—but it sure wasn't faith. The long-term consequences from what she pushed Abraham to do would have been unfathomable to her. But we are reminded of it every day when we see the hostilities between Arabs and Jews in the Middle East. When we take matters into our own hands and try to manipulate God's will to get what we want, sometimes He allows it. Misery can result.

SARAH LAUGHS AT GOD

Thirteen years later, Sarah was not looking much better. God came to Abraham again to tell him that Sarah would have a son. "He said, 'I will surely return to you at this time next year; and behold, Sarah your wife will have a son.' And Sarah was listening at the tent door, which was behind him" (Genesis 18:10). At the time of this promise, Abraham was ninety-nine, and Sarah was eighty-nine. Having a child at their age was physically impossible, and Sarah knew it. She had been barren all her life—she was well past menopause. She seemed to be at peace with Hagar. Barrenness seemed to be her destiny.

Then God showed up, true to His word. Genesis 18:1–8 tells of three men appearing to Abraham:

> Now the LORD appeared to him by the oaks of Mamre, while he was sitting at the tent door in the heat of the day. When he lifted up his

eyes and looked, behold, three men were standing opposite him; and when he saw them, he ran from the tent door to meet them and bowed himself to the earth, and said, "My Lord, if now I have found favor in Your sight, please do not pass Your servant by. Please let a little water be brought and wash your feet, and rest yourselves under the tree; and I will bring a piece of bread, that you may refresh yourselves; after that you may go on, since you have visited your servant." And they said, "So do, as you have said."

So Abraham hurried into the tent to Sarah, and said, "Quickly, prepare three measures of fine flour, knead it and make bread cakes." Abraham also ran to the herd, and took a tender and choice calf and gave it to the servant, and he hurried to prepare it. He took curds and milk and the calf which he had prepared, and placed it before them; and he was standing by them under the tree as they ate.

Abraham practiced one of the great virtues in the Middle East: he showd hospitality to these strangers and invited them in. If ever there was a case of "entertaining angels unaware," this was it. Little did Abraham know that he was not just entertaining angels, but he was showing hospitality to the Lord Himself (Genesis 18:13). This was another one of the theophanies of the Old Testament. This was an appearance of Jesus to man—as a man—long before He was incarnated as a baby in Bethlehem.

How did Sarah respond to this good news? As any good cynic would. She wasn't born yesterday. All those years of an unrealized promise of God's word had made her hard. It wasn't going to happen. Heck, she might not even live another year, much less have a child. So she laughed as Abraham had when the Lord told him a year earlier that Sarah would have a child. Abraham and Sarah laughed at God's promise, not only because they probably felt they were near death's door, but do you think they were still sexually active at eighty-nine and ninety-nine years old? God's Word tells us what she was thinking: "Now Abraham and Sarah were old, advanced in age; Sarah was past childbearing. Sarah laughed to herself, saying, 'After I have become old, *shall I have pleasure*, my lord being old also?'" (Genesis 18:11–12; emphasis added). She was referring to Abraham as her lord, but the real Lord is Jesus, and He was not happy about her cynicism or her lack of faith. And make no mistake—cynicism toward God and His Word is always a sign of spiritual deadness.

The Lord confronted Sarah's laughter. He said, "Why did Sarah laugh, saying, 'Shall I indeed bear a child, when I am so old?' Is anything too difficult for the LORD? At the appointed time I will return to you, at this time next year, and Sarah will have a son" (Genesis 18:13–14).

God's response reminds us of the angel Gabriel's response to the virgin Mary when he told her she would give birth to God's Son, and she responded incredulously, "How can this be, since I am a virgin?" (Luke 1:34).Gabriel told her that she would supernaturally conceive by the power of the Holy Spirit, "for nothing will be impossible with God" (v. 37). There can be few statements that are more important about God. He is all-powerful. No matter how impossible His will seems to man, nothing is impossible for God. Real faith is believing this. Yet Sarah showed a lack of faith, for she responded to the humanly impossible like any seasoned cynic. This was not her finest hour.

Sarah made things worse when she overheard the Lord's response to her laughter and then lied about it. "Sarah denied it however, saying, 'I did not laugh'; for she was afraid. And He said, 'No, but you did laugh'" (Genesis 18:15). Lies follow sin, for lies seek to cover up sin. When confronted about wrong, we tend to lie and deny it, for we want to look better than we are. But God sees right through our lies—just as He did with Sarah. How embarrassing! The Lord had come to bring Abraham and Sarah the greatest news of their lives, and she laughed in cynical disbelief. Then when her cynicism was exposed, she lied about it. What a low moment in her life.

If Sarah's story stopped here, things would not look good for her. Yet in His amazing patience, in His inexplicable grace, God did not reject her. He still had great plans for Sarah. What encouragement for all of us when our faith is weak and we do things that disappoint God. How wonderful it is to know that our loving God still has great plans for our lives. And those plans are about transforming our hearts and lives where others can learn from our mistakes and faithlessness and yet be inspired at the person God transforms us to be.

God would do this with Sarah, but it wouldn't be overnight. It would take many years. He would have a lot of transforming to do.

SARAH'S NEW TYPE OF LAUGHTER

"Then the LORD took note of Sarah as He had said, and the LORD did for Sarah as He had promised" (Genesis 21:1). God kept His promise to Abraham and Sarah. He always does. His word is the ultimate in dependability. Keeping one's word is a rare commodity in our world. It is so appreciated when we see it in another, especially when people go to extraordinary lengths to keep their commitments.

One of my all-time favorite books and miniseries is *Lonesome Dove*. There are so many great scenes. One of them is near the end when Gus's best friend, Captain Call, finally arrives at Lonesome Dove, Texas, after bringing Gus's body all the way from Montana, where he had died. Gus had asked him to bury him at a favorite place by a river, and Captain Call said he would. The last part of the story is the extraordinary adventure of Captain Call's taking Gus's body back to Lonesome Dove. It made him a living legend in the mythical American West. Captain Call finally completed his journey and buried Gus where he promised he would—with tears in his eyes as he reflected on the life of his friend. He said, "Well, Gus; there you go. I guess this will teach me to be more careful about what I promise people in the future." It's a moment of humorous inspiration at the incredible price one man paid to keep his word. Oh, how the world longs for such men, but they are few and far between.

Yet there is One who always keeps His word. His promises are as sure as the sunrise at the beginning of each day. His name is God. "So Sarah conceived and bore a son to Abraham in his old age, at the appointed time of which God had spoken to him" (Genesis 21:2). God did what He said He would do, but it was at His appointed time—the perfect time.

Another miniseries that captivated the nation was *Roots*, by Alex Haley. This incredible story focused on the life of an American slave and his family, from the slave's perspective. It opened the eyes of many white people to the hardships of slavery in a way many had never imagined. During an interview following the series, a reporter asked Haley if he'd ever imagined his book would have such an impact after all these years. I'll never forget his response. He told of a visit to his grandmother's when he was a child. She was a godly woman of faith and said to him, "Alex, God doesn't always work on our time, but He's always on time."

Sarah and Abraham would agree. God gave them His long-promised child at His appointed time.

"Abraham called the name of his son who was born to him, whom Sarah bore to him, Isaac. Then Abraham circumcised his son Isaac when he was eight days old, as God had commanded him" (Genesis 21:3–4). When God kept His promise, Abraham did what God commanded him to do. He named him *Isaac*, which means "laughter," and then he had Isaac circumcised on the eighth day as a sign that he was the covenant child. God had kept His covenant with Abraham, and now Abraham obeyed God.

"Now Abraham was one hundred years old when his son Isaac was born to him. Sarah said, 'God has made laughter for me; everyone who hears will laugh with me.' And she said, 'Who would have said to Abraham that Sarah would nurse children? Yet I have borne him a son in his old age'" (Genesis 21:5–7). This time Sarah laughed differently. It was not a cynical laugh, mocking the word of God. It was a laugh of total joy and wonder at what God had done. It was the joy of having a child after all those years of barrenness. It was the joyous celebration of experiencing God's will after agonizing years of waiting. It was the joy of laughing *with* God—not *at* God.

God told Abraham to name their child Isaac to remind them He gets the last laugh when it comes to cynicism and doubt. Sarah had laughed at God in disbelief. Now she laughed with God in faith, realizing that God not only had blessed her with this child but also kept His promises.

On December 2, 2002, the *Atlanta Journal-Constitution* ran the headline "A Century of Strom Thurmond," an article on how the senior senator from the great state of South Carolina had celebrated his one hundredth birthday as the longest-serving US senator. They commented on the senator's ninetieth birthday ten years earlier. At his ninetieth birthday, some guests expressed hope that they would experience his one hundredth, to which Senator Thurmond had quipped, "If you eat right and exercise regularly, I don't see any reason why you shouldn't be around to see it."[3] A hundred years old and serving in the US Senate was extraordinary. But being one hundred years old and having a baby with a ninety-year-old woman? That's a miracle indeed!

Laughter filled the tent of Abraham and Sarah at the miracle God had done. Every time they uttered Isaac's name, it would be a reminder of how trustworthy God is. It would be a reminder of the amazing grace of God to transform their laughing *at* God to laughing *with* God.

But Sarah still had a long way to go in becoming the woman God created her to be.

SARAH'S LACK OF FAITH—AGAIN

"The child grew and was weaned, and Abraham made a great feast on the day that Isaac was weaned" (Genesis 21:8). In those days, children were weaned at about three years of age. When the time occurred, it called for a celebration. Isaac was no longer an infant; he was a child.

One day, Sarah saw Isaac's half brother mocking him—as older brothers tend to do. Isaac was about three; Ishmael was now a teenager. "Now Sarah saw the son of Hagar the Egyptian, whom she had borne to Abraham, mocking. Therefore she said to Abraham, 'Drive out this maid and her son, for the son of this maid shall not be an heir with my son Isaac.' The matter distressed Abraham greatly because of his son"

(Genesis 21:9–11). Watching Ishmael mocking Isaac made Sarah furious. Perhaps it conjured up painful memories of Hagar taunting Sarah's barrenness when she was pregnant with Ishmael.

Rather than responding maturely, Sarah responded furiously. Ishmael was a threat to her son, Isaac. Not just physically but from the fact that he was Abraham's oldest son. Even though Ishmael was not God's covenant child, Sarah worried that he might try to claim the special privileges of being Abraham's firstborn son. And I'm sure Ishmael's presence was an ongoing reminder of a time when she lacked faith and took matters into her own hands. With a combination of anger and fear and guilt and anxiety, she demanded that Abraham kick Hagar and Ishmael out of their household. This distressed Abraham greatly. He loved his elder son.

God told Abraham to do what Sarah said, for it was through Isaac that His promises would be realized. "God said to Abraham, 'Do not be distressed because of the lad and your maid; whatever Sarah tells you, listen to her, for through Isaac your descendants shall be named. And of the son of the maid I will make a nation also, because he is your descendant.' So Abraham rose early in the morning and took bread and a skin of water and gave them to Hagar, putting them on her shoulder, and gave her the boy, and sent her away. And she departed and wandered about in the wilderness of Beersheba" (Genesis 21:12–14). In His mercy and compassion for Hagar and Ishmael, God would bring a great nation from the seed of Ishmael as well. Abraham sadly but obediently did what God said. He sent Hagar and Ishmael away. He trusted God to once again keep His word—yet it pained him greatly.

Once again we have a greater understanding of the Middle East conflict today. The feuding of the sons of Isaac (Israel) and the sons of Ishmael (the Arabs) goes all the way back to a mom who believed God helps those who help themselves. The sons of Ishmael, the elder son of Abraham, feel that Ishmael got a raw deal. He was treated unjustly. Their resentment is understandable. Yet God's plan all along was to build the chosen people of faith through the seed of Isaac, the covenant child.

HAGAR THE MAID

Some people seem to get the shaft. Hagar was one of those people. We know Hagar was from Egypt. We know she was Sarah's maid. We know she became Abraham's concubine. And we know she gave birth to Abraham's oldest son, Ishmael. This created huge problems with Sarah and didn't make Abraham look too good either.

But the book of Genesis doesn't give us Hagar's background. How did she get from Egypt to the land of Canaan? She probably became the maid of Sarah when Abraham and Sarah passed through Egypt shortly after he had seen Canaan for the first time. After all, Pharaoh was so enamored with the beauty of Sarah that he gave Abraham "sheep and oxen and donkeys and male and *female servants*" (Genesis 12:16; emphasis added), in hopes of having her as his wife. It makes sense that Hagar would be one of those female servants. Or maybe she was a runaway slave who found her way to Canaan after fleeing Egypt. I wonder about this—since *Hagar* means "forsake," "retire," "emigration," or "stranger." Did she immigrate to Egypt and find her way to Abraham's household? We just don't know. There is a lot about this woman we don't know. But she definitely affected the course of history in the Middle East to this day.

We know nothing of Hagar's background or how she wound up in the household of Abraham and Sarah—but there she was—first mentioned in Genesis 16:1: "Now Sarai, Abram's wife had borne him no children, and she had an Egyptian maid whose name was Hagar." And from the moment she is mentioned, Hagar's life is out of her control.

HAGAR WAS POWERLESS

Hagar, as a maid, was also a servant to Sarah, perhaps a type of slave. In ancient culture, these people did not have rights. As a matter of fact, the American declaration that "all men are . . . endowed by their Creator with certain inalienable rights"[4] would have been so foreign to Hagar that the thought never fluttered through her brain. So Hagar was powerless, and people who are powerless often get the shaft from people in power over them. Such was the case for Hagar. When Sarah had the idea of Hagar sleeping with her husband to have a child through her, Hagar could do nothing to put the brakes on that idea. Like Thomas Jefferson's slave and concubine, Sally Hemings (in the ultimate irony, as he wrote the Declaration of Independence), Hagar may have liked the idea or it may have repulsed her—but she was powerless to do anything about it. She had no rights as Sarah's slave. The EEOC had not been invented. Sexual harassment by those in power over another was an unknown concept. So it was for Hagar—a woman who paved the way for surrogate motherhood. Only she was not paid to provide her services.

But Hagar got a break; she conceived with Abraham. For the first time in her life, this blessing gave her power over Sarah. Not legal power, but emotional power. And she milked it for all it was worth. She had something Sarah did not. She was able to do something Sarah had longed for all her adult life: carry Abraham's child. Her prideful expressions around Sarah threw her mistress into a rage. Sarah made her life so miserable that Hagar had to flee. She couldn't take it anymore. "But Abram said to Sarai, 'Behold, your maid is *in your power*; do to her what is good in your sight.' So Sarai treated her harshly, and she fled from her presence" (Genesis 16:6; emphasis added).

HAGAR WAS TREATED UNJUSTLY

Hagar did what Sarah wanted—but when she was successful with Sarah's idea, she was treated unfairly. So she left. Once again Hagar was living up to her name's meaning of "forsake," "retire," "emigration," or "stranger." Hagar didn't want the job, so she headed for home. But home meant going through a vast desert—the wilderness of Shur. If you have ever been to the Holy Land—to the wilderness that connects southern Israel to northeastern Egypt—you know that it is so stark and vast that the chances of anyone surviving on their own more than a few days would be slim. For a pregnant woman traveling alone—slim to none.

During her journey through the desert, Hagar stopped by a spring of water. The angel of the Lord appeared and asked her, "Hagar, Sarai's maid, where have you come from and where are you going?" (Genesis 16:8).

Always remember—when the Lord asks us a question, it is not because He doesn't know the answer. Of course God knew where Hagar had come from. He knew where she was going. But at this point I doubt Hagar had any idea she was talking to the angel of the Lord. He was just a strange man to her. But I do believe He startled her when He called her by name and identified her as Sarah's maid. Runaway slaves could get in big trouble. She answered Him honestly: "I am fleeing from the presence of my mistress Sarai" (Genesis 16:8). Then the angel of the Lord gave her a command: "Return to your mistress, and submit yourself to her authority" (v. 9). Now, that was the last thing Hagar wanted to hear from a strange man in the desert. Sarah was making her life miserable.

Then Hagar realized that this stranger was no ordinary man—or even an ordinary angel. Genesis 16:10 says, "Moreover, the angel of the LORD said to her, 'I will greatly multiply your descendants so that they will be too many to count.'" Angels don't have this power. Only God Himself has this kind of power. Here we go again—another theophany. Remember, so often in the Old Testament, the appearance of "the angel of the Lord" is a preincarnate appearance of Jesus Christ, who is the Creator of all.

What a prophecy! Here was this poor, powerless woman, miserable and alone in the desert with little hope, and God told her she would be the mother of many descendants—"too many to count." The angel of the Lord told her:

> Behold, you are with child,
> And you will bear a son [she didn't know that—they didn't have ultrasound in those days];
> And you shall call his name Ishmael ['God hears'],

Because the LORD *has given heed to your affliction.*
(Genesis 16:11)

Hagar must have been praying to Abraham's God. At the end of herself—
feeling totally powerless—she learned that the all-powerful God of the
universe heard her prayers. It's as though He hears us best when we come
to the end of ourselves—powerless with nowhere else to go.

The angel continued His description of Ishmael, the baby in Hagar's
womb:

He will be a wild donkey of a man [that's enough to make a first-time
mother gulp],
His hand will be against everyone,
And everyone's hand will be against him;
And he will live to the east of all his brothers. (Genesis 16:12)

What a prophecy for the heirs of Ishmael who would settle in the Arabian
desert—east of the land of Canaan. Restless Bedouin Arabs always on
the move with ongoing tribal conflict. Thousands of years later, one of
those Arabs—named Muhammad—exasperated this even more when
he founded Islam. His descendants, the Sunnis and Shiites, are battling it
out even now. Almost every day the news reports suicide bombings in the
Middle East—Shiites against Sunnis or Sunnis against Shiites or whomever
else they hate or has the misfortune of being in their way. The prophecy
continues to be fulfilled to this day.

Yet at that time Hagar knew that God was being merciful to her. She
called God "You are a God who sees," saying, "Have I even remained alive
here after seeing Him?" (Genesis 16:13). The woman who got the shaft
finally got a break. "So Hagar bore Abram a son; and Abram called the
name of his son, whom Hagar bore, Ishmael. Abram was eighty-six years
old when Hagar bore Ishmael to him" (Genesis 16:15–16).

Hagar believed the word of God, obeyed the word of God, and in
faith returned to Abraham and told him what God told her through the

angel. Abraham believed her and welcomed her back into their house-hold. Realizing that she had heard the word of God, Abraham named their son Ishmael.

Evidently things settled out between Hagar and Sarah. They made their peace or at least coexisted in the household for about sixteen years. Then three years after God gave Abraham and Sarah their long-promised covenant child, Isaac, the bad blood between Sarah and Hagar returned with a vengeance. On the day of Isaac's weaning party (the ancient equivalent of a child's birthday party), Sarah saw Hagar's son, Ishmael (then sixteen years old), mocking the three-year-old Isaac. It made Sarah's blood boil, and she demanded that Abraham kick Hagar and Ishmael out of the house. "Therefore she said to Abraham, 'Drive out this maid and her son, for the son of this maid shall not be an heir with my son Isaac'" (Genesis 21:10).

Abraham was not happy about kicking out his oldest son, and he knew it was unfair to Hagar as well. But God told him to do what Sarah said. Humanly speaking, this was unfair. Sometimes what God may be leading us to do makes no sense at all at that time. It seemed wrong to Abraham, and it certainly seemed wrong to Hagar and Ishmael.

Teenagers are swift to point out what's unfair to their parents. I doubt Ishmael was any different. But God had His perfect plan for Abraham and Sarah and Isaac; and He had His permissive plan in sending Hagar and Ishmael out of the household because of Abraham and Sarah's sin. There Hagar and Ishmael would have to learn complete dependence on Him.

Abraham gave them some bread and water and sent them away. That's not much for surviving in the desert. Once again Hagar found herself in a hopeless and powerless situation. Once again Hagar and now her son got the shaft. Note what God's Word tells us: "When the water in the skin was used up, she left the boy under one of the bushes. Then she went and sat down opposite him, about a bowshot away, for she said, 'Do not let me see the boy die.' And she sat opposite him, and lifted up her voice and wept" (Genesis 21:15–16). She felt hopeless and was waiting to die.

Yet once again God's Word reminds us that when we come to the end of ourselves, He goes to work most dramatically. Hagar was weeping and waiting to die when God called to her from heaven. "What is the matter with you, Hagar?" (Genesis 21:17). Remember, God never asks a question that He does not know the answer to—but I bet it ticked her off. She probably said something like, "What's the matter? *What's the matter?* We are sitting here about to die because we've been treated so unfairly and You ask, what's the matter?"

Then God said, "'Do not fear, for God has heard the voice of the lad where he is. Arise, lift up the lad, and hold him by the hand, for I will make a great nation of him.' Then God opened her eyes and she saw a well of water; and she went and filled the skin with water and gave the lad a drink" (Genesis 21:17–19). Ishmael—"God hears." How could she forget—especially when God ministered to her fifteen years before when she was in a similar plight? But Hagar, like all of us, forgot how God met her needs in the past when she focused on the present circumstance that overwhelmed her. Circumstances and problems can blind us to God's faithfulness. They give us spiritual amnesia.

God told Hagar to go take the hand of her son and lift him up, and He reminded her of the promise He made to her sixteen years earlier when He told her He would bless her with more descendants than she could count through Ishmael. Then God led her to water and met their immediate needs, as He would every day of their lives. Evidently He wanted Hagar and Ishmael to trust Him day by day. Sure enough, God met their needs and watched over them, and Ishmael grew up to become a strong, "untamable" man.

Lessons from Two Women

God keeps His word. His promises are true. It happened with Abraham and Sarah and it would happen with Hagar and Ishmael. Sometimes His timing is not the timing we would choose. We tend to become impatient and cynical and lose faith. But God's timing is always perfect—He is always on time for His appointed time.

Self-help religion is not true faith. Believing Benjamin Franklin more than God's Word can create a heap of problems and complications. The bottom line is that acting in the flesh with good intentions to help God out is not faith. It is sin. Faith is the persistent belief in God and His Word.

When we sin, God is merciful and compassionate to keep working in our lives to fulfill His ultimate plans. Yes, there are consequences of our sin. God doesn't remove those. When Abraham and Sarah acted with the philosophy of "God helps those who help themselves," it resulted in long-term consequences in the Middle East that we can see today.

But God is also merciful to those victimized by sin, like Hagar and Ishmael. Ishmael's birth was not as God had planned, but when it occurred, God gave His word that He would build a great nation from Ishmael as well.

> *A father of the fatherless and a judge for the widows,*
> *Is God in His holy habitation.*
> *God makes a home for the lonely.* (Psalm 68:5–6)

When God fulfills His promise, especially when it is a long time coming, it brings great joy. Joy of wonder. Joy of gratitude. Joy at His grace—that in spite of our shortcomings and lapses of faith and sin, His sovereign plan will be done.

Sarah had lots of weaknesses, but in the end, God transformed her into a true woman of faith. In the new covenant, Sarah is described this way: "By faith even Sarah herself received ability to conceive, even beyond the proper time of life, since she considered Him faithful who had promised. Therefore there was born even of one man, and him as good as dead at that, as many descendants AS THE STARS OF HEAVEN IN NUMBER, AND INNUMER-ABLE AS THE SAND WHICH IS BY THE SEASHORE" (Hebrews 11:11–12).

If it can happen with Sarah, it can happen with us. But in the meantime, we can save ourselves and others lots of grief the sooner we learn to trust God's Word more than Ben Franklin's.

4

SIBLING RIVALRY
Isaac and Ishmael

*The child grew and was weaned, and Abraham made a great feast
on the day that Isaac was weaned. Now Sarah saw the son
of Hagar the Egyptian, whom she had borne to Abraham, mocking.*

—GENESIS 21:8—9

Have you ever struggled with sibling rivalry, whether your own or your kids'? It seems more pronounced among same-sex siblings close in age, and it is often exaggerated by perceived injustice of one being shown favor over the other. Every parent of more than one child has heard one of their children scream, "It's not fair." And sometimes it's not. Life can be very unfair. Sibling rivalry can lead to jealousy, anger, resentment, hatred, vengeance, and worst of all, murder. After all, sibling rivalry is as old as man.

The very first family, Adam and Eve, had two sons. The elder son, Cain, murdered his younger brother, Abel, in a vengeful rage because he felt unfairly treated by God. Why? Because God approved of Abel's sacrifice and not of Cain's (Genesis 4:1–8). The jealous resentment of Cain in the very first family represents sibling rivalry at its worst.

Yet sibling rivalry is dicier and often more divisive within the blended family. Children living under the same roof with half-siblings—who have one parent in common, but not the other—often feel they are jockeying for position. Perceived slights and unfairness are aggravated when the stepchild of one parent feels that his stepparent is treating his natural child with more favor. More than 50 percent of the children in America's public schools come from single-parent homes.[1] That's a setup for exacerbated difficulties when it comes to sibling rivalry.

Blended families in today's world give the best understanding of what it was like to grow up in polygamous families—same dad, different moms. That is the type of family Isaac and Ishmael lived in for a short few years—and the impact of the sibling rivalry between these two half brothers is still reverberating daily in the Middle East conflict.

RIVALRY BEGINS WITH CONCEPTION

The seeds of turmoil of this sibling rivalry began with their conception. It is explained in the new covenant book of Galatians, penned by the apostle Paul. "For it is written that Abraham had two sons, one by the bondwoman and one by the free woman. But the son by the bondwoman was born according to the flesh, and the son by the free woman through the promise" (Galatians 4:22–23). Isaac was the long-awaited promised child—the child of God planned to fulfill His covenant to Abraham of bringing forth a great nation. Ishmael was born in the flesh when Sarah believed she needed to help God out with His plans when she was well beyond childbearing years.

Isaac's conception was supernatural; Ishmael's was natural. Isaac's conception came about through faith; Ishmael's through a lack of faith. Isaac's conception proved the trustworthiness of God's Word; Ishmael's conception showed Sarah and Abraham's lack of trust in God's Word.

Isaac's conception is a reminder of how God desires the family to grow; Ishmael's conception reflects a family that results from man's sin. The contrast in their conceptions could not be starker. It was a natural setup for conflict that would lead to jealousy, resentment, insecurity, and rejection. It is an eternal reminder from God's Word to trust Him and wait on His timing versus taking matters into our own hands.

Rivalry Is Understandable

Ishmael's resentment of his younger brother was understandable. Ishmael was conceived through no fault of his own. As we have seen, his birth came about because of the accepted practice in the ancient world of allowing a barren woman's husband to sleep with his wife's servant in order to have a legal heir. Though the practice was legal and accepted, it was never God's will for Abraham and Sarah. Polygamy and surrogate motherhood were never God's original intent for marriage and the family.

God's design for marriage is clearly described in the first marriage of Adam and Eve. When God (the original Father of the bride) created Eve out of Adam and brought her to him, Adam was thrilled. Then God said, "For this reason a man shall leave his father and his mother, and be joined to his wife; and they shall become one flesh" (Genesis 2:24). God is clear—His intention for marriage is for one man with one woman. Not one man and several women. Not one man with another man. Not one woman with several men. God's intention is for one man and one woman only—as long as they both shall live.

Jesus reiterated this design when He was asked about divorce. He responded by talking about marriage:

> Some Pharisees came to Jesus, testing Him and asking, "Is it lawful for a man to divorce his wife for any reason at all?" And He answered and said, "Have you not read that He who created them from the beginning MADE THEM MALE AND FEMALE, and said, 'FOR THIS REASON A MAN

SHALL LEAVE HIS FATHER AND MOTHER AND BE JOINED TO HIS WIFE, AND THE TWO SHALL BECOME ONE FLESH'? So they are no longer two, but one flesh. What therefore God has joined together, let no man separate" (Matthew 19:3–6).

The religious leaders wanted to know when divorce was allowed. Jesus' response spoke to the sanctity of marriage. He knew divorce was never God's original intention. It was only allowed because of men's hard hearts of sin. Then Jesus quoted Genesis 2:24: God designed marriage for one man with one woman. Period.

So poor Ishmael was a victim of man's sin from the moment of his conception. His birth was not God's best plan for Sarah, but He allowed it because of their weakness of faith.

EXPECTED FIRSTBORN FAVOR

Ishmael, as the elder child, certainly expected special favor. Traditionally in the ancient world, the elder son was given preferential treatment. He would receive more honor, more responsibility, and two shares of the family inheritance versus one for all other siblings.[2] Later Mosaic Law would legalize this preferential treatment in Deuteronomy 21:17: "But he shall acknowledge the firstborn, the son of the unloved, by giving him a double portion of all that he has, for he is the beginning of his strength; to him belongs the right of the firstborn." Ishmael probably realized this at a young age. It's likely that when he would meet adult friends of Abraham, many would smile and say something like, "Ah, the elder son—you shall be doubly blessed." So Ishmael grew up with a sense of entitlement as Abraham's elder son—even if it was only perceived in his mind.

For thirteen years, Ishmael was Abraham's only son. They had to have a special relationship. Remember, when God came to Abraham and reiterated His promise to give him his long-awaited promised son, Abraham not only fell on his face with skeptical laughter at the human impossibility of he and Sarah having a child together, but he added, "Oh that Ishmael might live before You!" (Genesis 17:18) Abraham's response reveals not only a lack of faith in God's promise, but a natural affinity he had developed for Ishmael, his oldest son. I'm sure Ishmael perceived that.

THE BREAKING POINT

As we saw in the previous chapter, the sibling rivalry came to the breaking point when Ishmael was sixteen and Isaac was about three. "The child [Isaac] grew and was weaned, and Abraham made a great feast on the day that Isaac was weaned" (Genesis 21:8). In the ancient world, a child was weaned around three years old, and a great family celebration occurred.[3] The child was now moving from infancy to childhood. It was a celebration because so many children died in infancy. If the child lived this long, there was a good chance he would live to adulthood.

Ishmael, at sixteen, was old enough to know that because Isaac was born to Sarah, Abraham's wife, and not his mother, Hagar, Sarah's maid, Isaac had special status in the home. This had to make Ishmael's "elder son" status feel insecure. So on this big day in Isaac's life, Ishmael mocked him as big brothers tend to do to their little brothers—especially when they feel their younger siblings are receiving too much attention.

Sarah saw it and she was furious. "Now Sarah saw the son of Hagar the Egyptian, whom she had borne to Abraham, mocking. Therefore she said to Abraham, 'Drive out this maid and her son, for the son of this maid shall not be an heir with my son Isaac'" (Genesis 21:9–10). Ishmael, as the elder son, was a threat to her son's future status. He also was a living reminder of her prior lack of faith in God's promises. With a combination of "mama bear" protection and guilt over her earlier lack of faith for God's will to be fulfilled, Sarah reacted to Ishmael's laughing with passionate fury. He and his mother, her longtime faithful servant, had to go.

Abraham was not happy about it. "The matter distressed Abraham greatly because of his son" (Genesis 21:11). He loved Ishmael. He knew this was unfair to him and his mother. Yet amazingly God agreed with Sarah and told Abraham, "Do not be distressed because of the lad and your maid; whatever Sarah tells you, listen to her, for through Isaac your descendants shall be named. And of the son of the maid I will make a nation also, because he is your descendant" (Genesis 21:12–13).

Now put yourself in Ishmael's sandals. Here is a sixteen-year-old son who loves his dad—and all of a sudden, he is being kicked out of his home. We are talking injustice—big-time. Can't you see Ishmael responding, "It's not fair! I'm your oldest son! I can't believe you're doing this to me in favor of that little squirt."

My wife and I have three sons. Like most parents, we tended to be more lenient with our younger kids. How many times have we heard our older sons say, "It's not fair" when their younger brother got to do things they never did! Yet Abraham did this out of obedience and trust in God's Word and a desire to please his wife.

Nothing will infuriate teenagers like being treated unjustly by a parent and then being rejected by a parent. Just ask any child of divorce when one parent deserts them. It's a slight many adult children still feel bitterness over throughout their adult life. But what adds fuel to the fire of resentment is when a son sees his mama treated badly by his dad. "So Abraham rose early in the morning and took bread and a skin of water and gave them to Hagar, putting them on her shoulder, and gave her the boy, and sent her away. And she departed and wandered about in the wilderness of Beersheba. When the water in the skin was used up, she left the boy under one of the bushes. Then she went and sat down opposite him, about a bowshot away, for she said, 'Do not let me see the boy die.' And she sat opposite him, and lifted up her voice and wept" (Genesis 21:14–16). Can you imagine how this young man felt seeing his mother treated this way? Imagine his helpless fury in not being able to do anything to help her in a time of despair as the water ran out, and they were waiting to die in the desert.

God had prophesied to Hagar that her son would be a "wild donkey of a man." At age sixteen, Ishmael probably already had a restless and insecure spirit—ready to fight at any perceived slight. But imagine the impact of this rejection by his father. I think he was furious at how his dad had treated his mom. It's little wonder how God's prophecy for Ishmael's life and his heirs would be magnified. His whole life and heritage would be fueled by resentment and rage at how he and his mother were treated so unjustly. His descendants (the Arabs) would pick up on it and inherit this anger and resentment of the sibling rivalry with Isaac and his heirs (the Jews) that lingers on to this day. From Ishmael came the Arabs. From Isaac came the Jews.

ISAAC, THE COVENANT CHILD

God kept His promise. He always does. His Word is trustworthy. It was always God's plan for Isaac to be the covenant child. Abraham and Sarah had a hard time believing it—they were too old!—but God's plan will prevail. "Then the LORD took note of Sarah as He had said, and the LORD did for Sarah as He had promised. So Sarah conceived and bore a son to Abraham in his old age, at the appointed time of which God had spoken to him. Abraham called the name of his son who was born to him, whom Sarah bore to him, Isaac" (Genesis 21:1–3). Isaac's birth reminds the people of faith that when God's Word says it's going to happen, it's going to happen. When we face insurmountable challenges and problems in life, this is a huge encouragement and comfort.

The seed of Abraham through Sarah would be used by God to build a great nation—a covenant people—one day called Israel. God didn't choose Hagar and Ishmael for this task through a man-made scheme to help God out. God didn't choose Egypt—the most powerful nation on earth—through the gift of a son to Pharaoh. God chose an obscure couple with extraordinary faith to begin to fulfill His promise to Abraham that He would build a great nation through his seed. God came to Abraham once again to reassure him when He said of Sarah in Genesis 17:16: "I will bless her, and indeed I will give you a son by her." Abraham couldn't believe it and even laughed about the absurdity of it, since he was ninety-nine and Sarah was eighty-nine. Yet God kept His word and fulfilled His promise. So He does with all His followers who trust Him and believe in the promises of His Word.

NOTHING IS IMPOSSIBLE WITH GOD

Isaac's birth reminds us nothing is impossible with God. When I came to be the first pastor of our church, we had about twenty families meeting in an empty doctor's office. We had no building of our own, though we had put a down payment on some property in a great location in our community. Near the end of that first year in 1982, we were a couple of months away from our first annual land payment that would allow the bank to release the property for construction of our first permanent facility for worship. The clock was ticking, and we needed more than fifty thousand dollars by the end of the year. We gave all the children a dollar bill and told them the parable of the talents—urging them to take the Lord's dollar and go multiply it and bring the proceeds back to the Lord the Sunday before our land payment was due. We asked each family to begin to pray about what the Lord was leading them to give in cash that same Sunday. I remember that my wife and I came to a very odd number.

The Sunday the special offering was due, the twenty or thirty children gave several hundred dollars that they had earned by investing the dollar given to them, through jobs such as buying gasoline to mow lawns or buying raw materials to make crafts to sell in their neighborhoods. There was a spirit of excitement and anticipation in the air. At the end of the service, the finance chairman announced that the church had given *to the exact dollar* what was needed for the land payment. We gasped, and for a moment there was total silence. No one could say a thing. When God moves supernaturally—unexplainably—there is a holy awe that leaves us speechless. As we tried to comprehend the fact that God had done the impossible by leading each person to give the exact amount needed to meet the goal—including the several hundred dollars by the children—we were stunned. It galvanized the faith of our young congregation and said to us that God definitely wanted a new church in our community. Scripture reminds us in the recorded history of the supernatural birth of Isaac that nothing is impossible with God.

When Isaac was about twelve, God called on Abraham to sacrifice the boy. Remember this was the son through whom God had promised to build a great nation. "Now it came about after these things, that God tested Abraham, and said to him, 'Abraham!' And he said, 'Here I am.' He said, 'Take now your son, your only son, whom you love, Isaac, and go to the land of Moriah, and offer him there as a burnt offering on one of the mountains of which I will tell you'" (Genesis 22:1–2).

This scriptural passage tells an excruciating story that is hard for any parent to grasp. God never intended for Abraham to sacrifice his son; He just wanted to see if Abraham would put Him before his son. He wanted to see if he was willing to let go of his greatest blessing from God, one that was central to the fulfillment of God's promises. Abraham showed that he loved God by obeying Him, and at the last moment God told him to stop. "But the angel of the LORD called to him from heaven and said, 'Abraham, Abraham!' And he said, 'Here I am.' He said, 'Do not stretch out your hand against the lad, and do nothing to him; for now I know that you fear God, since you have not withheld your son, your only son, from Me'" (Genesis 22:11–12).

After God stopped Abraham, He provided a ram for him to sacrifice in place of his son. Then God reiterated the promise.

Then the angel of the LORD called to Abraham a second time from heaven, and said, "By Myself I have sworn, declares the LORD, because you have done this thing and have not withheld your son, your only son, indeed I will greatly bless you, and I will greatly *multiply your seed* as the stars of the heavens and as the sand which is on the seashore; and your seed shall possess the gate of their enemies. *In your seed* all the nations of the earth shall be blessed, because you have obeyed My voice." (Genesis 22:15–18; emphasis added)

Abraham had great faith—but so did Isaac, in being willing to be sacrificed in obedience to his Father's will. What a foreshadowing of things to come.

A Foreshadowing

In many ways Isaac's life foreshadows the life of Christ. Both were the sons promised to their earthly parents by an angel of the Lord. Both were supernaturally conceived, showing nothing is impossible with God. Both were long-promised sons through whom God would build a people of faith. Both were born to be a blessing to the nations. In the willingness to be sacrificed to fulfill his father's will, Isaac foreshadowed the sacrifice of Jesus on the cross to fulfill His Father's will. And both were covenant children. Isaac was used by God to begin the old covenant with God's people. Jesus was sent by God to begin the new covenant with all people who trust in Him.

God's plans for Isaac and Jesus did indeed become a blessing to the nations.

Isaac and Ishmael Brought Together

Yet God's plans for Isaac were very different from His plans for Ishmael. After about seventy-two years of separation and estrangement, Isaac and Ishmael were brought together again. It came at Abraham's death. "These are all the years of Abraham's life that he lived, one hundred and seventy-five years. Abraham breathed his last and died in a ripe old age, an old man and satisfied with life; and he was gathered to his people. Then his sons Isaac and Ishmael buried him in the cave of Machpelah, in the field of Ephron the son of Zohar the Hittite, facing Mamre" (Genesis 25:7–9). Many times in preparation for a funeral, the family of the deceased gathers in my office before the service. Several times a family member has quietly pointed out a sibling or a child he or she hasn't seen or spoken to in years, but the death of a parent has brought them together again. I always feel sadness in my heart at all those lost years of estrangement. Such was the case for Isaac and Ishmael. Isaac finally meets the brother he barely knew. He was seventy-five, and Ishmael was eighty-eight. How do you think Isaac and Ishmael felt that day after all those years of separation? Sadly, their coming together would be short-lived. No lasting reconciliation took place. Their heirs in the Middle East are a continual testimony to that to this day.

In December 2003, a woman named Essie May Washington was introduced to the American public. She was a seventy-eight-year-old retired Californian schoolteacher. What made her story so remarkable was she was the unknown daughter of the late Senator Strom Thurmond of South Carolina, who had recently died at one hundred years old. Thurmond made his career as an arch-segregationist governor and the longest-serving US senator in American history. What made it even more sensational was Essie May is black. When I was at the University of South Carolina in the early 1970s, people joked about "Old Strom" being like Abraham when he married his second wife when she was in her early twenties and he was in his sixties. He wound up having four children by his second wife. But little did we know how much "Old Strom" was like Abraham. Earlier in life, he had fathered his first child by the black maid of his wealthy family. After his death in December 2003, his child made herself known and surprised the reporters in that she had no bitterness. Unlike Abraham with Ishmael, "Old Strom" had kept in touch with her and helped meet her financial needs all the way through college.

Abraham did none of that. As a matter of fact, at Abraham's funeral, God's Word said he left everything to Isaac. "It came about after the death of Abraham, that God blessed his son Isaac; and Isaac lived by Beer-lahai-roi" (Genesis 25:11). After all those years of estrangement, Ishmael showed up at his father's funeral and got the shaft again. How do you think he felt? How do you think his sons felt in hearing his story as they settled in Arabia as the Bible documents in Genesis 25:12–18?

Interestingly, as history has unfolded, the resentment seems more focused on Isaac and his heirs than it does on Father Abraham. Among

Islamic Arabs, Abraham is viewed fondly as the father of their faith. But they greatly resent the heirs of Isaac (Israel and the Jews). That resentment only intensified in 1948 when the United Nations awarded Israel a homeland in Palestine, just over thirteen hundred years after the heirs of Ishmael had claimed it when the Muslim Arabs conquered Jerusalem.

Once again Ishmael's heirs were furious and deeply resentful at the heirs of Isaac. It all seemed so unfair. And it all started with a sibling rivalry many years ago that originated with their father's sin, a sobering reminder of the long-term consequences of one man's sin.

5

PLAYING FAVORITES
Isaac and Rebekah, Esau and Jacob

Now Isaac loved Esau, because he had a taste
for game, but Rebekah loved Jacob.

—GENESIS 25:28

If you have more than one child, you know the temptation to play favorites. This is a natural tendency because children are people, and we are more drawn to certain people than others. But parental favoritism is a temptation no parent wants to give in to. It will create tension and resentment not only in the parent-child relationship but also among the siblings. That was certainly the case for Isaac's children.

Abraham's son Isaac found a beautiful wife named Rebekah. Technically, his father's faithful servant found her for him—but Isaac loved the choice. She was a honey. From the day Isaac saw Rebekah, it was love at first sight. He had waited forty years to get married, and it was totally worth it. "And he took Rebekah, and she became his wife, and he loved her" (Genesis 24:67).

But Isaac and Rebekah had a problem. Like so many of the great women of faith in the Bible, Rebekah was barren. They went twenty years without having a child. This is a problem, for God promised Isaac's father that He would bring forth a great nation from his seed. That meant not only would he and Sarah need to have a son, but their heir would need to have a son as well. Now, twenty years into Isaac's marriage, there was no heir, no child, no son.

Yet unlike his father and mother, Isaac didn't make the mistake of taking matters into his own hands, trying to help God out. He did the right thing: he prayed for God to "open the womb" of his wife, Rebekah, and then he waited on God to do what He had promised. God answered Isaac's prayer, and Rebekah became pregnant. So far, so good.

But from the moment of conception there were problems. Medical science today is still bewildered why some women have miserable pregnancies and some don't. They wonder why some women with miserable pregnancies produce very healthy children, while others with an easy pregnancy have children with all sorts of health problems.

Pregnant with twins, Rebekah was in a lot of pain and discomfort. I'm sure she was thankful to be pregnant, but she was like all of us when we desperately want something and God blesses us with what we want—we face unexpected problems and cry, "Why?" With her unborn twins struggling within her, she asked God, "Why then am I this way?" (Genesis 25:22).

God responded, "Two nations are in your womb; / And two peoples will be separated from your body" (Genesis 25:23). He told her she was having twins. We don't know how God told her; He just did. But that's not all He told her. From these two twins would come two nations. Wow, that had to boggle the mind of a mother-to-be. This is quite a prophecy. The boys hadn't even been born yet, and God was telling her two nations would come from these two children. (It had to be two sons because in those days a new nation would never come from a woman. That would have been inconceivable.)

And there is more to God's prophecy: "One people shall be stronger than the other; / And the older shall serve the younger." (Genesis 25:23).

God revealed which one would have the stronger nation. What manifest destiny. God's Word prophesied to Rebekah not only about her pregnancy and having twins but the whole history of their heirs.

From this explanation comes the insight on her painful, troubled pregnancy. Those boys were jockeying for position even in their mother's womb. I've heard mothers say of their children, "They've been fighting since the day they were born." But I've never had a mother tell me, "They were fighting before they were born, and here's why."

The day for Rebekah to give birth finally arrived, and out came twin boys who could not have been more different. The first one was red and hairy all over at birth. So they name him Esau ["hairy"] (Genesis 25:25). The second son was just the opposite. He was smooth all over, and he didn't lack ambition. When Esau was born right before him, this second son was grabbing onto his heels. This explained the war in Rebekah's womb. That second child was determined to be first. Even though it appears that Esau won that battle, the second child was fighting it all the way. They named him Jacob, which means three things: "heel grabber," "cheater," and "supplanter." Esau was all boy, full of vim and vigor. He loved to hunt—a man's man. Jacob, on the other hand, liked the indoors and was a peaceful child.

Hey, guys! Who do you think you'd like best? An athlete—a man's man who loved the great outdoors—or a scheming mama's boy who liked to stay inside all day, helping his mama with the sewing and cooking? Your answer reveals why Isaac loved Esau but Rebekah loved Jacob.

We live in a culture where so many mothers and female schoolteachers make the mistake of favoring those little boys who are easy to manage. The rambunctious boys drive them crazy. They feel they are a problem. Too disruptive. Disinterested in learning. Why can't they be good students like the girls?

Rebekah obviously bought into this mind-set. She loved Jacob best, and Isaac loved Esau. Parental favoritism among two very different boys would send this sibling rivalry over the edge. It would not only fracture a family permanently, but it would also lead to exasperating the problems in the Middle East to this day.

JACOB'S AMBITION

One day, when Jacob and Esau were probably young teenagers, Esau came in from hunting absolutely famished. He saw that Jacob was cooking some red stew. Not one to worry with niceties like, "How ya doing, Jake?" he said, "Give me some of the red stuff." From this scene, this redheaded wooly bugger took on a second name—Edom, which means "red" (Genesis 25:30). Don't forget that name Edom. It is central to Esau's manifest destiny.

Jacob, ever the schemer, responded, "First, sell me your birthright." In those ancient families, the birthright of the firstborn usually meant a double portion of the inheritance for the elder son. On top of that he became the head of the family. Later, Mosaic Law would speak to this: "But he shall acknowledge the firstborn, the son of the unloved, by giving him a double portion of all that he has, for he is the beginning of his strength; to him belongs the right of the firstborn" (Deuteronomy 21:17).

Esau responded impulsively. He lived in the moment. Destiny? Who cares? He was more interested in the next meal or the next hunt or whatever satisfied the need for the moment. So he said, "Look. I'm about to starve to death. What good is a birthright to me dead?"

Jacob, ever calculating and plotting to look out for himself, said, "First swear to me." And Esau did (Genesis 25:33). To make an oath in the ancient world was like a written legal contract. It was irrevocable. Jacob got what he wanted, and so did Esau. Their bargain met Esau's immediate needs, but in the long run, it was a bad deal for him. He would come to regret it—big-time.

REBEKAH AND JACOB'S DECEPTION

Years later, when Isaac was old and blind and felt he was near death, he sent his beloved son, Esau, out to hunt. He hoped Esau would come back and prepare Isaac's favorite wild game meal so that he might bless him before he died. Esau, I'm sure, was more than happy to oblige. Any day he could be outdoors hunting was a good day for him. Besides, that scheming mama's boy brother of his had taken his birthright, so securing his father's blessing was important. Maybe, he thought, it might even overrule what he had committed to Jacob.

Isaac obviously showed favoritism to Esau, even though Rebekah had probably told him the prophecy of God concerning their twin boys. He still favored Esau, even though Esau had married foreign wives that about drove him and Rebekah batty. Isaac loved Esau most because they liked the same manly things, but Rebekah did not. She preferred Jacob and had God's prophetic word to back her up. When she overheard what Isaac requested of Esau—and planned to do—she went into action.

What is interesting is how similar Rebekah's mind-set was to Sarah's: when God's promises didn't seem to be working out, she took matters into her own hands. Again, we see the Ben Franklin approach to religion: "God helps those who help themselves." Only this scheme wasn't for her—this was for Jacob. Sarah's plan was at least socially acceptable. But Rebekah's plan involved telling her son to lie to his father in order to get what she and Jacob wanted. As sorry as Jacob was in living up to his name, in this case he shows a bit more decency in his fearful tendency than Rebekah did. Out of weakness, he would give in to her temptation. But knowing what an abuse of parental authority this was—what deception and lack of respect for her husband she showed—Rebekah's plans were scandalous. This is parental favoritism gone wild, and sadly, like so many severe cases of parental favoritism, it would destroy this family.

Here's what happened. It's a long passage of Scripture, but savor every morsel. Each verse and phrase writes a short story that cannot be matched by any of the great writers of modern literature. Hemingway, Twain, O'Connor—none can come close to the powerful drama chronicled by the biblical writer. Parental favoritism and sibling rivalry is a volatile mix:

> Now it came about, when Isaac was old and his eyes were too dim to see, that he called his older son Esau and said to him, "My son." And he said to him, "Here I am." Isaac said, "Behold now, I am old and I do

not know the day of my death. Now then, please take your gear, your quiver and your bow, and go out to the field and hunt game for me; and prepare a savory dish for me such as I love, and bring it to me that I may eat, so that my soul may bless you before I die."

Rebekah was listening while Isaac spoke to his son Esau. So when Esau went to the field to hunt for game to bring home, Rebekah said to her son Jacob, "Behold, I heard your father speak to your brother Esau, saying, 'Bring me some game and prepare a savory dish for me, that I may eat, and bless you in the presence of the LORD before my death.' Now therefore, my son, listen to me as I command you. Go now to the flock and bring me two choice young goats from there, that I may prepare them as a savory dish for your father, such as he loves. Then you shall bring it to your father, that he may eat, so that he may bless you before his death."

Jacob answered his mother Rebekah, "Behold, Esau my brother is a hairy man and I am a smooth man. Perhaps my father will feel me, then I will be as a deceiver in his sight, and I will bring upon myself a curse and not a blessing." But his mother said to him, "Your curse be on me, my son; only obey my voice, and go, get them for me."

So he went and got them, and brought them to his mother; and his mother made savory food such as his father loved. Then Rebekah took the best garments of Esau her elder son, which were with her in the house, and put them on Jacob her younger son. And she put the skins of the young goats on his hands and on the smooth part of his neck. She also gave the savory food and the bread, which she had made, to her son Jacob.

Then he came to his father and said, "My father." And he said, "Here I am. Who are you, my son?" Jacob said to his father, "I am Esau your firstborn; I have done as you told me. Get up, please, sit and eat of my game, that you may bless me." Isaac said to his son, "How is it that you have it so quickly, my son?" And he said, "Because the LORD your God caused it to happen to me." Then Isaac said to Jacob, "Please come close, that I may feel you, my son, whether you are really my son Esau or not."

So Jacob came close to Isaac his father, and he felt him and said,

"The voice is the voice of Jacob, but the hands are the hands of Esau." He did not recognize him, because his hands were hairy like his brother Esau's hands; so he blessed him. And he said, "Are you really my son Esau?" And he said, "I am."

So he said, "Bring it to me, and I will eat of my son's game, that I may bless you." And he brought it to him, and he ate; he also brought him wine and he drank. Then his father Isaac said to him, "Please come close and kiss me, my son." So he came close and kissed him; and when he smelled the smell of his garments, he blessed him and said,

> "See, the smell of my son
> Is like the smell of a field which the LORD has blessed;
> Now may God give you of the dew of heaven,
> And of the fatness of the earth,
> And an abundance of grain and new wine;
> May peoples serve you,
> And nations bow down to you;
> Be master of your brothers,
> And may your mother's sons bow down to you.
> Cursed be those who curse you,
> And blessed be those who bless you."

Now it came about, as soon as Isaac had finished blessing Jacob, and Jacob had hardly gone out from the presence of Isaac his father, that Esau his brother came in from his hunting. Then he also made savory food, and brought it to his father; and he said to his father, "Let my father arise and eat of his son's game, that you may bless me." Isaac his father said to him, "Who are you?" And he said, "I am your son, your firstborn, Esau."

Then Isaac trembled violently, and said, "Who was he then that hunted game and brought it to me, so that I ate of all of it before you came, and blessed him? Yes, and he shall be blessed." When Esau heard the words of his father, he cried out with an exceedingly great and bitter cry, and said to his father, "Bless me, even me also, O my father!" And he said, "Your brother came deceitfully and has taken away your blessing." Then he said, "Is he not rightly named Jacob, for he has supplanted me these two times? He took away my birthright, and behold, now he has taken away my blessing." And he said, "Have you not reserved a blessing for me?"

But Isaac replied to Esau, "Behold, I have made him your master, and all his relatives I have given to him as servants; and with grain and new wine I have sustained him. Now as for you then, what can I do, my son?" Esau said to his father, "Do you have only one blessing, my father? Bless me, even me also, O my father." So Esau lifted his voice and wept. Then Isaac his father answered and said to him,

"Behold, away from the fertility of the earth shall be your dwelling,
And away from the dew of heaven from above.
By your sword you shall live,
And your brother you shall serve;
But it shall come about when you become restless,
That you will break his yoke from your neck."

So Esau bore a grudge against Jacob because of the blessing with which his father had blessed him; and Esau said to himself, "The days of mourning for my father are near; then I will kill my brother Jacob."

Now when the words of her elder son Esau were reported to Rebekah, she sent and called her younger son Jacob, and said to him, "Behold your brother Esau is consoling himself concerning you by planning to kill you. Now therefore, my son, obey my voice, and arise, flee to Haran, to my brother Laban! Stay with him a few days, until your brother's fury subsides, until your brother's anger against you subsides and he forgets what you did to him. Then I will send and get you from there. Why should I be bereaved of you both in one day?" (Genesis 27:1–45)

Then Rebekah pleaded with Isaac to send Jacob away to her native land so that he might find a wife from her homeland. And Isaac agreed.

Wow! What drama. What intensity. Rebekah's scheming. Jacob's lying. Isaac's trembling. Esau's weeping. Esau's plans for vengeance. Jacob's fleeing. No soap opera could outdo this. No literature could describe it more powerfully!

REBEKAH'S AMBITION FOR JACOB

Most parents want the best for their children, and many parents have great hopes for their children. But it's hard to grasp Rebekah's parental ambition and favoritism toward Jacob. First of all, Rebekah commanded her son to deceive his father to get what they both wanted. This is pure parental abuse, commanding her child to plot and scheme with her to do evil. Parents who are so ambitious for their children that they teach them to lie and steal to get what they want are the embodiment of evil.

Second, Rebekah was so ambitious for Jacob that she was willing to be damned to get what she wanted (Genesis 27:12–13). William Manchester's biography of Douglas MacArthur, *The American Caesar*, tells how his mother was so ambitious for him that when he enrolled at West Point, she rented an apartment nearby so she could see if his dorm room light was on late at night to know if he was studying to be tops in his class.[1] That is another mother who was over-the-top in ambition for her son. No wonder the man's ego was gigantic.

Mothers like MacArthur's may occasionally produce great sons, but they sure can be hard to take. But I doubt these types of mothers would ever proclaim that they were willing to spend eternity in hell to get what they wanted for their son, as Rebekah did. It is a picture of ambition for her son that is difficult to grasp.

AN IRREVOCABLE OATH

In Isaac's day, the father's blessing was like an oath. It was irrevocable—like a written will in today's world. After Isaac blessed Jacob, thinking he was Esau, and then Esau returned and Isaac realized he had been deceived, God's Word says, "Then Isaac trembled violently" (Genesis 27:33). These four words graphically tell the horror of this scene—as a blind, elderly father realizes he has been deceived and there is nothing he can do about it. The oath has been made—the contract was irrevocable.

He had been deceived by his own son, and I believe he sensed his wife was behind it. He had seen her favoritism through the years. He could not bless the son he wanted to. He felt like a fool. It says he trembled violently. In four short words, the biblical writer reveals that Isaac perceived everything even though he could not see.

In the movie *Braveheart*, King Edward of England despised and abused the Scots all through his reign. Little did he know his daughter-in-law had fallen in love with William Wallace, the Scottish revolutionary warrior who, for many years, heroically led Scotland in rebellion against King Edward. While the king was on his deathbed, so weak he was unable to speak, his daughter-in-law whispered in his ear that she was carrying the child of William Wallace. Edward's heir would be a Scotsman. King Edward trembled violently in his bed, for there was nothing he could do about it. Oh the horror of a parent, deceived by a child and the results are opposite of what the parent wants, and the parent can do nothing about it.

Esau's Impulsiveness

Esau's impulsive, live-for-the-moment mind-set brought bitter results. "When Esau heard the words of his father, he cried out with an exceedingly great and bitter cry, and said to his father, 'Bless me, even me also, O my father!' ... Do you have only one blessing, my father? Bless me, even me also, O my father.' So Esau lifted his voice and wept" (Genesis 27:34, 38). So Esau bore a grudge in this sibling rivalry and vowed to kill his brother for what he had done. Esau, a grown man, cried like a little child feeling treated unjustly because of parental favoritism: "It's not fair!" Desire for revenge quickly followed.

After helping Jacob deceive his father, Rebekah kept on lying and scheming. She manipulated Isaac to send Jacob away to find a wife. When Esau saw that he was outfoxed one more time by his mother and Jacob, he left home and took another wife from the heirs of Ishmael. Notice that Ishmael reappears in this story. His heirs have a way of showing up when

Abraham's heirs, who feel they are being treated unfairly, get angry at God and life. It would later be Ishmaelites who showed up when Jacob's beloved son Joseph was sold into slavery by his brothers, who were jealous of him because his father loved Joseph most. Ishmaelites purchased Joseph and sold him into slavery in Egypt (Genesis 37:28).

Rebekah loved Jacob. Isaac loved Esau. Yet because of parental favoritism and sibling rivalry, they would never see their sons again. Parental favoritism caused each of them to lose the child they loved most. Those are long-term consequences. Jacob and Esau would be estranged for more than twenty years. But there would be even more long-term consequences from these sins within the family, affecting the turmoil in the Middle East today.

6

REAPING WHAT YOU SOW
Jacob and the Birth of Israel

God said to him, / "Your name is Jacob; / You shall no longer be called Jacob, / But Israel shall be your name." / Thus He called him Israel.

—GENESIS 35:10

I t might be hard to understand, but God chose to bless Jacob over Esau. From his attempt at being born first, to his participation in his mother's scheme to steal the blessing, he truly lived up to the other meanings of his name—"supplanter," "cheater," and "deceiver." He was a lying, scheming mama's boy.

But here is what is amazing—God had great plans for Jacob, and I mean great plans. Plans that would shape the course of history. And this is extremely encouraging because if God can love Jacob, He can love anybody. He can even love you and me. It not only gives us hope for ourselves; it gives us hope for those sorry characters in the world who are like Jacob.

So how did God shape Jacob into the man He wanted him to be? How would Jacob's life shape the course of history and influence events in the Middle East? It would take a long time.

A RENEWAL OF THE PROMISE

After Rebekah and Isaac sent Jacob away (because Esau wanted to kill him), God appeared to Jacob in a dream. For many years I wished God would speak to me in a dream, like He often did to great biblical characters. As I've matured, I'm so thankful He doesn't because so many of my dreams are wildly bizarre! Thankfully, I forget most of my crazy dreams within a few seconds of waking.

Yet with many biblical characters, God used dreams over and over. Why? Sometimes He did so when there was no written word of God that was adequate for guidance in His will. The revelation of God was unfolding in Jacob's life, but it was not yet recorded. Moses is generally believed to be the writer of the first five books of the Bible. He would live more than four hundred years after the life of Jacob. So when Jacob was headed to the former homeland of his father and grandfather to find a wife, God's revelation of His plan and His will for him came through a dream.

It was a strange dream. Jacob "had a dream, and behold, a ladder was set on the earth with its top reaching to heaven; and behold, the angels of God were ascending and descending on it" (Genesis 28:12). A ladder going up to heaven with angels going up and down on it? What is this all about? As the dream unfolded, God spoke to Jacob in a way that gave him interpretation of the dream.

> And behold, the LORD stood above it and said, "I am the LORD, the God of your father Abraham and the God of Isaac; the land on which you lie, I will give it to you and to your descendants. Your descendants will also be like the dust of the earth, and you will spread out to the west and to the east and to the north and to the south; and in you and in your descendants shall all the families of the earth be blessed. Behold, I am with you and will keep you wherever you go, and will bring you back to this land; for I will not leave you until I have done what I have promised you." (Genesis 28:13–15)

What was God saying to Jacob in this dream?

First of all, God was saying, "I'm over all of history." That meant God was over the plans of Jacob's life. He stood atop this ladder that ascended to heaven, and His angels would be going back and forth from heaven to earth and earth to heaven orchestrating God's plans.

Second, a key part of God's plans for history would involve Jacob's forefathers and his heirs. It was a revelation of the covenant promise of God made to his grandfather, Abraham, and his father, Isaac. Jacob was God's chosen heir of this covenant. God reiterated these promises to him:

- He would give his descendants the land (Genesis 28:13).
- He would make the descendants of Abraham—Isaac and now Jacob—more than anyone could count (Genesis 28:14).
- Through this specially chosen family, God would bless all the families of the earth (Genesis 28:14).
- God would be with him and watch over him and would one day bring him back to this promised land (Genesis 28:15).

Obviously Jacob didn't deserve this. His character up to this point was despicable. Yet what a reminder from God to us all—if God has a purpose for a guy like Jacob, He certainly has a purpose for all of us. No, it would not be easy. It would take a long time. God was not only patient with Jacob, like He is with all of us, but He would use painful lessons to shape Jacob's character.

JACOB MEETS HIS MATCH

When I was growing up and some sorry so-and-so got caught for doing wrong and was in a heap of trouble, I would often hear an adult say, "Well, I guess he got what was coming to him." Even though I was just a child, I clearly understood that the troublemaker was reaping what he had sown by getting in serious trouble. It meant that most everyone who knew the sorry character was not a bit surprised that person had gotten caught and was getting what he deserved.

In Genesis 29, God's Word tells how Jacob had traveled hundreds of miles east to the land of his mother. Travel was not easy in those days. The roads were bad, and there were no convenience stores with restrooms like today. Yet Jacob arrived at his mother's hometown and stopped by a well. Wells often served as the service stations of ancient times. They were a place to water the camels—the SUVs of ancient Israel—and a place for Jacob to get a drink as well. It was not uncommon for people to gather around the wells, enjoying a much-needed pit stop in what could be incredibly hot and tiring travel. But in this case the stone that covered the well to keep it clean was so heavy it took several men to move it. When the guys at the well told him he was at his destination, Haran, Jacob had to be relieved. Then he was downright astounded that they knew his relative by the name of Laban. About that time they looked up and said, "There is his daughter Rachel coming with the sheep," for she was a shepherdess.

This was a scene out of Hollywood. God's Word describes it vividly in Genesis 29:10–11: "When Jacob saw Rachel the daughter of Laban his mother's brother, and the sheep of Laban his mother's brother, Jacob went up and rolled the stone from the mouth of the well and watered the flock of Laban his mother's brother. Then Jacob kissed Rachel, and lifted his voice and wept." We are talking love at first sight. Here was this mama's boy seeing this beautiful young woman, and he was so inspired that he was empowered with incredible strength. He did something that normally took the strength of several men to do. He moved the huge stone off the top of the well all by himself—so Rachel could water her flocks. Then he ran up to her and kissed her and began to weep. Then he told her where he was from and how they were distant cousins. Now, that was some scene. Rachel was so taken aback that she hightailed it home to tell her daddy what had happened at the well.

Laban invited Jacob to spend a month with them. Then he officially introduced Jacob to his two daughters. The older was named Leah. The younger was Rachel. This is what God's Word tells us about the two daughters: "Now Laban had two daughters; the name of the older was Leah, and the name of the younger was Rachel. And Leah's eyes were weak, but Rachel was beautiful of form and face" (Genesis 29:16–17). Leah had weak eyes. In a culture where the women usually wore veils so the only part of a woman's face a man might see was her eyes, this was not good. Weak eyes were not just about eyesight but about her looks, and poor Leah was lacking in that department. But Rachel was a babe. I'd call her a honey—but young men today would say she was a hottie. The Word of God couldn't be clearer. This gal was a looker. What a body—what a beauty. To add insult to injury for Leah—Leah's name meant "cow." Rachel meant "lamb." Poor Leah. Life was tough enough being the unattractive, badly named older sister, but on top of that she had a gorgeous younger sister.

One thing about Jacob: when he saw something he wanted, he was totally focused and determined. He had found the woman of his dreams. He offered to work for Laban for seven years for the right to marry Rachel. Laban agreed.

The seven years flew by for Jacob. The Bible says it "seemed to him but a few days because of his love for her [Rachel]" (Genesis 29:20). When seven years were complete, Jacob went to Laban and bluntly said, "Give me my wife, for my time is completed, that I may go in to her." Wow. He was demanding that his future father-in-law give Rachel to him in marriage so he could finally have sex with her. Nothing subtle here.

So Laban threw a big wedding party; but unbeknownst to Jacob, Laban pulled a fast one on him. Weddings would usually be held at night. The bride would be heavily veiled. As the wedding party extended late into the night, the wine would flow freely. So being a schemer himself and being a man who knew the prospects of his older daughter getting married were not good, Laban brought Leah to be married to Jacob. Jacob evidently didn't know, and he consummated the marriage with Leah, thinking he was doing so with Rachel. "Laban gathered all the men of the place and made a feast. Now in the evening he took his daughter Leah, and brought her to him; and Jacob went in to her . . . So it came about in the morning that, behold, it was Leah! And he said to Laban, 'What is this you have done to me? Was it not for Rachel that I served with you? Why then have you deceived me?'" (Genesis 29:22–25).

Can you imagine the scene? Jacob thinking he was spending the night with the girl of his dreams. "Oh, Rachel—you are the most beautiful woman I've ever seen. I love you so. The wait has been so worth it." Then the next morning he rolls over to gaze at his beautiful bride, and "ol' weak eyes" is staring at him. Imagine how shocked he was. Imagine how poor Leah felt. This was not a happy scene. God's Word describes the irony of what follows: "'Why then have you deceived me?' But Laban said, 'It is not the practice in our place to marry off the younger before the firstborn. Complete the week of this one, and we will give you the other also for the service which you shall serve with me for another seven years.' Jacob did so and completed her week, and he gave him his daughter Rachel as his wife" (Genesis 29:25–28).

Jacob was furious that Laban *deceived* him. How ironic that the deceiver gets deceived. And double irony that Jacob had deceived his own father into thinking that he was the firstborn. Now Laban deceives Jacob by giving him his firstborn. Jacob the schemer got a taste of his own medicine, and he was furious. Jacob had met his match when it came to deception. Yet he was so in love with Rachel and so determined to marry her that he agreed to serve Laban on his ranch another seven years. Most people think Jacob had to wait another seven years to marry Rachel. He didn't have to wait seven more years to marry Rachel. He just had to wait a week, but he was obligated to serve his father-in-law for another seven years (Genesis 29:27–28).

Those of us who hear a story like this probably laugh at the fact that Jacob got what he deserved from Laban. No doubt he did. But God was using all the experiences of Jacob's life to shape him into the man He wanted him to be. The Bible says, "Do not be deceived, God is not mocked; for whatever a man sows, this he will also reap" (Galatians 6:7).

A rowdy bunch of teenagers were having fun on the land of a wealthy Southern farmer. The farmer had worked hard to have a fruitful harvest and didn't want rowdy teenagers out there damaging his crops, so he ran them off the land. The ringleader of the teens came up with an idea of how to get even with the old farmer. He and his buds sneaked into the farmer's fields one night and planted all kinds of kudzu. If you've ever lived in the South, you know kudzu grows faster than antlers on a buck. It will take over fields, trees, houses. It is an almost unstoppable leafy vine. Over the next couple of years, the teenagers watched from a distance and laughed as the farmer battled the kudzu continuously. A couple of years later, the ringleader of the group fell in love with the farmer's daughter. He received permission of the farmer to marry her. Soon the farmer died, and the young man inherited the family farm—only to battle kudzu the rest of his life.

Watch out how we treat others. God is not mocked. He'll see to it that in time we will reap what we sow. God is just, and He wants us to learn that the way we treat others is the way we are likely to be treated as well. Jacob was learning a hard lesson but a good lesson—for God had great plans for his life.

WRESTLING WITH GOD

In Genesis 29:24–32, we read how Jacob met his match with Laban. Then after years of service to him, Jacob finally had enough and took his two wives, Laban's daughters, and fled while Laban was away (Genesis 31:1–21). Because no deceiver wants to be outfoxed by another, when Laban heard about it, he was furious and pursued Jacob and his daughters and confronted him for leaving him. This was Jacob's response: "These twenty years I have been in your house; I served you fourteen years for your two daughters and six years for your flock, and you changed my wages ten times. If the God of my father, the God of Abraham, and the fear of Isaac, had not been for me, surely now you would have sent me away empty-handed. God has seen my affliction and the toil of my hands, so He rendered judgment last night" (Genesis 31:41–42). Finally Laban let them go. Jacob was becoming a man. But he still had a long way to go.

This led Jacob to face what he had been dreading for more than twenty years. He had to return home through the land his brother, Esau, and his heirs, the Edomites, had settled (Genesis 32:1–23). Guilt is haunting. Part of Shakespeare's genius was writing tragedies that caused the reader to grasp the vivid power of guilt. I'll never forget reading *Macbeth* in college and picturing Lady Macbeth constantly washing her guilty, murderous hands. Guilt is the curse of sin. Dostoevsky's *Crime and Punishment* describes it vividly as the main character, Raskolnikov, obsessively grasps the bloody sock after he has murdered a pawnbroker for money. Guilt is like a haunting, unshakable glue to our souls. We can try and run from it, but it's like a sack of sand sealed to our backs—it weighs us down wherever we go.

No matter how long Jacob had been gone, no matter how far he traveled and what he accomplished, he never got away from the guilt of what he had done to his brother, Esau, by deceiving his dad. Now he was about to come face-to-face with Esau after all those years of separation.

On the night before he was to face Esau, Jacob was all alone. Then Jacob had a life-changing encounter with the One he had sinned against most. Not Esau. Not his father. But God Himself (Genesis 32:24–32).

Jacob was confronted in the darkness by an unknown man, and he wrestled with the man all night long. Jacob didn't realize that he was wrestling with the Lord. In this long night of agony, I believe Jacob finally came face-to-face with his sin. Yes, he got a taste of it when he was deceived by Laban, but no one brings us so face-to-face with the evil of our sinful depravity like the Lord. It is then that we see ourselves and our sins as God sees them. Until we are convicted by our sin and potential for evil, it is impossible to begin to be transformed by the power of God. It is humbling and in some cases absolutely terrifying. This is why the slave trader John Newton, haunted by the guilt of making money trading human flesh, would one day write, "'Twas grace that taught my heart to fear, 'twas grace my fears relieved." God sometimes takes us through what theologians call "the dark night of the soul" so that when we see how sinful we are and see that God still loves us and offers us His forgiveness, in Christ we are forever changed.

God's Word describes this type of night for Jacob. "Then Jacob was left alone, and a man wrestled with him until daybreak" (Genesis 32:24). I can imagine Jacob's exhaustion. My dark night of the soul occurred in my bedroom at home the summer after my freshman year of college. I had been blessed with the spiritual high of being a student leader at the same Young Life ranch in Colorado where I had made a personal commitment to Christ two years earlier. But I was troubled. What did God want me to do with my life? I didn't know, but I distinctly remember kneeling by my bed before going to bed that night and praying, "Lord, I'm Yours—whatever You want me to do with my life, I'm willing." Then I got into bed to go to sleep. Only sleep never came. I began to wrestle with evil thoughts that I never thought I was capable of. I felt temptation all around me, and it became so intense I felt the devil was right next to me all night long, urging me to turn my back on God. I felt he was continually whispering in my ear, "Deny God—deny Jesus—turn your back on God." I kept resisting intensely, "No. No, I will not." It became terrifying. I didn't think I could hold out. I didn't sleep a wink.

Finally, after what seemed an eternity, morning came, and I got dressed to go to work. I walked down to the kitchen, and Mom asked what I wanted for breakfast. I was absolutely exhausted, and I couldn't eat. My dad looked up from reading the paper and asked, "How'd you sleep, son?" I burst into tears and blurted out, "I feel like I've been wrestling with the devil all night long." My parents were stunned, bewildered, and troubled to have their oldest son, home from college, respond that way. They didn't know what to say or do.

I stayed troubled for months. After the terror of that one night, I was fearful to go to bed at night. But God knew I needed it. He knew that an overly self-confident Christian college kid needed to be broken. I needed to have an awareness of the kind of evil and sin I was capable of. After that experience, I've known to this day that the most sinful person I've ever known is myself. That night I came to realize what I've never forgotten: I am capable of any sin, and only by the grace of God do I have the strength and power to overcome sin. Yes, God knew I needed that all-night wrestling match for my soul to be totally broken and to learn total dependence on Him. What I learned that night was that my determination to do right in my own strength would be too weak against the evil one. My intention was good, but my self-reliant strength couldn't face that battle with grit and determination day after day. It would be too much. At the end of myself, all I could do was learn to depend on the strength of God moment by moment. Thankfully, His strength is always sufficient by the power of the Holy Spirit.

I realize Jacob's experience was different. No dark night of the soul is exactly the same. He felt he was wrestling all night long with the Lord, not the devil. But the sense of spiritual wrestling and coming to the end of our strength through brokenness is similar. Jacob was riddled with guilt and fear in a time in his life when he was brought face-to-face with his sin. His wrestling match with the Lord for control of his life led to physical and spiritual brokenness that changed his life—his character—his spirit—his name forever. God's Word describes it in Genesis 32:25–32:

> When he [the angel] saw that he had not prevailed against him [Jacob], he touched the socket of his thigh; so the socket of Jacob's thigh was dislocated while he wrestled with him. Then he said, "Let me go, for the dawn is breaking." But he said, "I will not let you go unless you bless me."
>
> So he said to him, "What is your name?" And he said, "Jacob."
>
> He said, "Your name shall no longer be Jacob, but Israel; for you have striven with God and with men and have prevailed."
>
> Then Jacob asked him and said, "Please tell me your name." But he said, "Why is it that you ask my name?" And he blessed him there.
>
> So Jacob named the place Peniel, for he said, "I have seen God face to face, yet my life has been preserved."
>
> Now the sun rose upon him just as he crossed over Penuel, and he was limping on his thigh.
>
> Therefore, to this day the sons of Israel do not eat the sinew of the hip which is on the socket of the thigh, because he touched the socket of Jacob's thigh in the sinew of the hip.

First of all, Jacob was physically broken. His all-night wrestling match was so exhausting, his hip was dislocated. He would walk with a limp.

Second, Jacob's strength and determination are astounding. After wrestling all night long, he told this messenger of God he'd not let him go until he blessed him. The messenger of God asked his name, and when Jacob replied, "Jacob," he knew his name described who he was—supplanter, schemer, and deceiver. It was then this messenger or angel of God gave him a new name. He named him Israel, meaning "God rules" and "he strives against God."[1] The name would certainly foreshadow the history of Israel. Jacob wrestled with God and survived. Jacob begged the strong man to tell him his name, but the man refused and instead blessed him. This describes the mystery of God and His redemption of a sinful man all at once.

Finally, it is at this point that I believe Jacob was transformed by God. He realized he had had a supernatural encounter with God. He'd been guilt-ridden and terrified over his sin. When stating his name, he was overwhelmingly convicted of who he was. Yet rather than receiving the death and judgment of God he deserved, Jacob's name was changed by God, and God blessed him. Jacob would never be the same. Now he would be Israel—a new man. And from this new man would come a great nation that God had envisioned through his grandfather, Abraham. Out of Jacob, Israel was born. For even though Jacob thought he had prevailed, God had prevailed to change him and begin a specially chosen people and race.

JACOB AND ESAU MEET

Once Jacob experienced his dark night of the soul of "wrestling with God," he no longer held the fear he may have had in the past. God had prepared him for this moment. Yet even then, Jacob's calculating nature is displayed: "Then Jacob lifted his eyes and looked, and behold, Esau was coming, and four hundred men with him. So he divided the children among Leah and Rachel and the two maids. He put the maids and their children in front, and Leah and her children next, and Rachel and Joseph last" (Genesis 33:1–2). He sent his wives out to meet Esau and his four hundred men before he did. Maybe he thought seeing his family would soften Esau's heart. But what Jacob did next would have been unfathomable for him twenty years earlier. He showed the utmost humility and respect for Esau by bowing before him to the ground seven times. "But he himself passed on ahead of them and bowed down to the ground seven times, until he came near to his brother" (Genesis 33:3).

In the first year of President Obama's presidency, Americans were bewildered to see him bow before the king of Saudi Arabia. What did this mean—an American president bowing before the king of one of the most oppressive Muslim nations in the world? Then later that year, Obama was pictured bowing more deeply to the emperor of Japan as he met world leaders on his Asian tour.[2] Why did he do this?

In the Eastern world, the deeper a man bows before another, the greater the show of respect. So when Jacob bowed all the way to the ground before Esau, this was a picture of a new Jacob. Humbled by God, he was seeking Esau's forgiveness while putting himself at Esau's mercy.

Once again, the natural response of the reader toward Esau is very positive. After all that Jacob had done to him twenty years earlier, Esau was incredibly forgiving:

> Then Esau ran to meet him [Jacob] and embraced him, and fell on his neck and kissed him, and they wept. He lifted his eyes and saw the women and the children, and said, "Who are these with you?" So he said, "The children whom God has graciously given your servant." Then the maids came near with their children, and they bowed down. Leah likewise came near with her children and they bowed down; and afterward Joseph came near with Rachel, and they bowed down. And he said, "What do you mean by all this company which I have met?" And he said, "To find favor in the sight of my lord." But Esau said, "I have plenty, my brother; let what you have be your own." (Genesis 33:4–9)

Jacob felt he should offer Esau great gifts because he had treated him badly years before. But Esau was incredibly gracious and forgiving.

How did Jacob respond? "'No, please, if now I have found favor in your sight, then take my present from my hand, for I see your face as one sees the face of God, and you have received me favorably. Please take my gift which has been brought to you, because God has dealt graciously with me, and because I have plenty.' Thus he urged him and he took it" (Genesis 33:10–11). Through Esau's forgiveness, Jacob felt he was seeing the face of God and experiencing God's forgiveness. In many ways Esau resembles the father in Jesus' story of the prodigal son, showing us the forgiveness of God. So Jacob insisted Esau at least take gifts, and Esau did.

The brothers went their separate ways in peace. And along the way, God reiterated to Jacob that He was serious about changing his name.

Then God appeared to Jacob again when he came from Paddan-aram, and He blessed him. God said to him,

"*Your name is Jacob;*
You shall no longer be called Jacob,
But Israel shall be your name."

Thus He called him Israel. (Genesis 35:9–10)

God went on to repeat His earlier promise made to Jacob's grandfather and father and now him—that from Israel would come a great nation and the land He promised to Abraham and Isaac would be the land of Israel. From Israel came twelve sons, who would represent the twelve tribes of Israel (Genesis 35:23–26). From Esau came many heirs as well, described in Genesis 36.

THE EDOMITE'S HEIRS

Jacob and Esau's reconciliation was genuine. When their father, Isaac, died, the brothers came together once again. But as is often the case, the heirs of those who felt their father got the shaft are not so forgiving. Such would be the case for Esau's heirs, the Edomites.

As history unfolds, they would bitterly disappoint the Israelites. The Edomites were definitely their cousins, yet close relatives can often become bitter enemies. More than four hundred years later, when the Israelites were set free from slavery in Egypt and on their way to the promised land as a new nation, the Edomites would not let them pass through their land. The Edomites wound up settling south of Arabia in what is modern-day Jordan. Later, King Saul and King David of Israel waged war against the Edomites. Great Hebrew prophets like Amos (1:1–12), Isaiah (chapter 34), Jeremiah (49:7–22), Ezekiel (32:29), and Obadiah (entire book) condemn Edom for the way they joined with Israel's enemies against them. What was especially galling to Israel was how Edom was in cahoots with Babylon in the fall of Jerusalem in 587–86 BC.[3] To understand some of the tension with modern-day Israel and Jordan, one has to go all the way back to Jacob and Esau.

Later, when Christ was born, Herod—the hated king of the Jews who ordered all the babies of Bethlehem to be savagely murdered—was half-Jew and half-Edomite. Because he was part Edomite, as well as because of his appointment by Rome, he was resented by Israel.

Fast-forward about two thousand years to 1948, when Israel became a nation once again. Among the five Arab nations who declared war against Israel—to drive the Jews into the sea before the infant nation ever got under way—was Jordan, the nation filled with the Edomite heirs of Esau. But what is little known is what occurred three days before Israel became a nation and Arab neighbors declared war on Israel. On May 11, 1948, an American Jew by the name of Golda Meyerson (disguised as an Arab woman) held a secret meeting with King Abdullah of Transjordan (Jordan). The world would later know her as Golda Meir, who would become prime minister of Israel. Shimon Apisdorf wrote of the clandestine encounter, "It was Mrs. Meyerson's perception, as well as the perception of other Jewish and Arab leaders, that King Abdullah believed that a way could be found for Jews and Arabs to live as neighbors. On that day in May her mission was to dissuade the king from going to war. The king, for his part, told Mrs. Meyerson that it was impossible for him to break ranks with other Arab leaders and he urged the Jews to postpone their declaration of independence."[4] Sadly, Mrs. Meyerson had to return to David Ben-Gurion, the leader of Israel, and report her mission as a failure.

But she recorded what King Abdullah said to her that day: "I firmly believe that Divine Providence has restored you, a Semite people who were banished to Europe and have benefitted from its progress, to the Semite East, which needs your knowledge and initiative . . . I deplore the coming bloodshed and destruction. Let us hope we shall meet again and will not sever our relations."[5]

It is hard not to think of Esau and Jacob's reconciliation in Genesis 33. Two estranged brothers being reconciled and Esau's magnanimous forgiveness. It seems King Abdullah lived with that longing once again. Historically, the band of brothers known as Arabs was too strong to reconcile the heirs of Jacob and Esau, but the sentiment was there.

Then in 1967, in six days, little bitty Israel defeated five large Arab nations around them and claimed control of the sacred temple mount on which the Muslim Dome of the Rock sits. It was taken from Jordan, who had ownership of the land along with East Jerusalem and the land known every day in the news as the West Bank. It is called that, for it is on the "west side" of Jordan. To the Jordanians, the Edomite heirs of Esau, the sons of Jacob (Israel) were stealing from them again. One simply can't understand the tensions in the Middle East today unless one goes back to the origin of the conflict in biblical times.

Israel and Jordan are now, surprisingly, at peace. The late King Hussein of Jordan, the son of King Abdullah, realized Israel's right to exist and courageously signed a peace treaty with Israel as President Sadat of Egypt had done years earlier. Jordan has certainly been one of the more progressive Muslim regimes to work favorably with Israel and the US. Though King Hussein had lost much to Israel, and from his standpoint had been treated unjustly, his attitude toward Israel in the end was more like Esau with Jacob when he forgave him. Those who are for peace miss this courageous Muslim leader.

Time will tell how long this peace treaty will last. There is a very troubling verse in Romans 9:13 where God says, "JACOB I LOVED, BUT ESAU I HATED." To anyone who trusts in God as a just God, this verse is hard to take. But God's Word goes on to say that God can show favor to whomever He wants. It is in no way based on merit. Jacob sure didn't deserve it. Neither does Israel. Neither did Esau—or Jordan—or any of us.

7

A MIRACULOUS RESTORATION
The State of Israel and Neighboring Arab Nations

Therefore thus says the LORD *of hosts, "Because you have not obeyed My words,*
behold, I will send and take all the families of the north," declares the LORD,
"and I will send to Nebuchadnezzar king of Babylon, My servant, and
will bring them against this land and against its inhabitants."

—JEREMIAH 25: 8—9

I'll never forget the first trip my wife and I took to Israel. It was October 1991, and our Jewish guide had not led a tour group in a year and a half because of the Gulf War. We had a small group of nineteen people. Very few in our church were interested in going. News reports of Saddam Hussein's scud missiles falling on Israel were still weighing heavily on American minds. Pictures on CNN of Israelis stocking up on gas masks because of the fear of Saddam's Iraq striking Israel with chemical weapons did not enhance Americans' desires to go to that part of the world. Yet the moment our plane touched down in Tel Aviv, we knew we were in a place like no other. A large group of Irish Catholics on our plane began to sing the Doxology. That just doesn't happen anywhere else in the world.

Everywhere we went, Israelis were appreciative we had come. Yes, it was partly economic, but it was more. The presence of Americans showed our support to a beleaguered people who had not only been attacked in the Gulf War but all through history. All the boasting of Saddam Hussein against Israel had failed. Once again Israel had survived.

Even though most Americans felt Saddam's attacks on Israel were a ploy to seek to unify the Arab Muslim world under his leadership against the US in the Gulf War, it was not as simple as that. Part of his motivation was to lead Iraq back to the glory of ancient Babylon under their mightiest ruler—Nebuchadnezzar, who ruled over Babylon from 602–562 BC. There is quite a history between Babylon (modern-day Iraq) and Israel. It flows out of the history of Israel with the great powers of the ancient world.

EGYPT AND ISRAEL

The first great power was Egypt. In the ancient world, no kingdom was as great as Egypt. Their dynasty began in 3100 BC and didn't officially end until the Persians defeated them in 343 BC. During their days of world dominance, one of Jacob's (Israel's) sons, Joseph, was sold into slavery by his brothers to the Ishmaelites (Genesis 37:28), who would later sell him to the Egyptians. If ever there is a question of how God orchestrates events in history, just read the story of Joseph in Genesis 37–50. The nomadic heirs of Ishmael showed up and became the middlemen for selling Joseph into slavery in Egypt. God is the behind-the-scenes director of this divine drama as Joseph moves from being a trusted slave to a falsely accused slave to a prisoner to the prime minister of Egypt, answerable only to Pharaoh. "What man initiates for evil, God can turn into a means for good" (Genesis 50:20, author's paraphrase). Joseph believed this. While in the role of prime minister, Joseph became the savior of Egypt and Israel through wise planning to get them through a seven-year famine. Israel and all his sons had come to Egypt for food and stayed there.

But over time, Pharaohs of Egypt arose who "did not know Joseph" (Exodus 1:8). Eventually Egyptians enslaved the Israelites. This slavery would last about four hundred years. God finally intervened through his specially prepared, chosen leader, Moses, to set the people of Israel free from slavery and begin the journey to the land God had promised them. This was clearly prophesied by God to Abraham more than four hundred years earlier: "God said to Abram, 'Know for certain that your descendants will be strangers in a land that is not theirs, where they will be enslaved and oppressed four hundred years. But I will also judge the nation whom they will serve, and afterward they will come out with many possessions'" (Genesis 15:13–14). When God used Moses to set the children of Israel free from slavery, it foreshadowed what Jesus does for the individual who trusts in Him. He sets us free from slavery to sin so we can begin our journey to the ultimate promised land of heaven. The Jews remember their salvation from Egypt through the feast of Passover, when each household sacrificed the best lamb they had and spread the blood of the lamb on the doorposts of their houses. They did this so that when the angel of death passed over Egypt to bring judgment on Egypt with the death of the firstborn in every household, the angel sent by God would "pass over" the households of faith, the enslaved Jews. This final plague of judgment on Egypt was sent by God because of their stubborn, hard-hearted refusal to trust Israel's God and let His people go.

In God's perfect timing, Jesus and His Jewish disciples observed the Passover meal the night before He was crucified. This began the first Christian parallel with the ancient feasts of Israel. Christians observe the Eucharist, or Lord's Supper, knowing that Jesus is the Lamb of God, who was sacrificed to set us free from enslavement to sin. Trusting in Him through His shed blood saves us from God's judgment and death just as trusting in God through the Passover lamb saved Israel. God set Israel free from long-term enslavement in Egypt, and God has set the Christian free from enslavement to sin.

Egypt and Israel, Christ and Christianity—the historical connection is very real. This is why, when Anwar Sadat of Egypt and Menachem Begin of Israel signed a peace treaty known as the Camp David Accords during the presidency of professing Christian Jimmy Carter, Egyptians, Jews, and Christians all were amazed as was anyone with knowledge of biblical history. It was the one shining light of the presidency of Jimmy Carter.

Later when President Sadat, a Muslim, flew to Israel and spoke before Israel's house of Parliament, the Knesset, the world was doubly astounded in light of the history of Egypt and Israel. The courage of Anwar Sadat was unbelievable. Sadly, it would cost Sadat his life at the hands of Muslims who felt he had betrayed them. Fortunately, the Camp David Accords have mostly held firm under Sadat's successor, Hosni Mubarak, and a long line of Israeli prime ministers.

ANCIENT KINGDOMS THAT CHALLENGED EGYPT

It is true that no ancient kingdom compares in longevity of greatness to Egypt. Since Egypt, dominant worldly kingdoms have had a much shorter shelf life. The Hittites, out of what is modern-day Turkey and Syria, challenged Egypt's world dominance in the fourteenth and thirteenth centuries BC.[1] These are one of the many people groups inhabiting ancient Canaan (the promised land) when Abraham was led there by God. As a matter of fact, Abraham's first official claim to the land is described in Genesis 23:10–15:

> Now Ephron was sitting among the sons of Heth; and Ephron the Hittite answered Abraham in the hearing of the sons of Heth; even of all who went in at the gate of his city, saying, "No, my lord, hear me; I give you the field, and I give you the cave that is in it. In the presence of the sons of my people I give it to you; bury your dead."
>
> And Abraham bowed before the people of the land. He spoke to Ephron in the hearing of the people of the land, saying, "If you will only

please listen to me; I will give the price of the field, accept it from me that I may bury my dead there." Then Ephron answered Abraham, saying to him, "My lord, listen to me; a piece of land worth four hundred shekels of silver, what is that between me and you? So bury your dead."

It was from the Hittites that Abraham purchased some land around Hebron to bury his wife Sarah for four hundred shekels of silver. Hebron is a very dangerous place today. Israeli Jews and Palestinian Muslims both feel connected to Abraham there, and bitter violence has taken place over the ownership of the land.

The Hittites challenged Egypt for a time, but they soon faded in importance. Then came the Ethiopians, described in the Bible as the land of Cush, who conquered Egypt for a short period of time (715 BC–671 BC).[2]

Then the Assyrians invaded Egypt in 671 BC and sacked key cities in Egypt. For the next fifty years, Assyria and Egypt vied for world dominance. Historians still argue over who was the strongest as they battled back and forth. If you want to get the picture, think of the Soviet Empire's short-lived challenge to the US for world dominance in the twentieth century.

Yet Assyria is important, for they became an important part of biblical history during the period of Israel's and Judah's kings. These are described mostly in the books of 1 and 2 Kings and the parallel book of 2 Chronicles. Many Old Testament prophets rail against Assyria, yet the best-known example of a Jewish prophet speaking to the Assyrian kingdom was Jonah. He was called by God to preach in the Assyrian capital of Nineveh. He didn't want the job and boarded a ship headed west rather than going east toward Nineveh. Jonah was running from God. Yet he found out that nowhere on earth can we get away from God as God used a storm at sea and a mighty big fish to give Jonah a time of thoughtful reflection to consider the foolishness of his plans. Now, that's a whopper of a fish story. But it's true. Jesus spoke of it as historical fact in Matthew 12:38–41.

Finally, Jonah headed east to the great city of Nineveh and preached a one-sentence sermon: "Yet forty days and Nineveh will be overthrown" (Jonah 3:4). Much to Jonah's dismay, the people of Nineveh repented and God forgave them. Jonah, like all Jews, having suffered at the hands of Assyria, wanted God to bring judgment on them. He became that rare preacher who is depressed and angry when an evil, sinful people responded to his sermon of warning and judgment through repentant faith. If you haven't read Jonah in a while, it's not just a big fish story; it is a fun and humorous read that reminds us of the awesome power of God through a very human and reluctant prophet. Go ahead; put down this book and read it. It's just four chapters. You can read it in a few minutes. You'll love it.

The Assyrians were a powerful kingdom headquartered in what is now northern Iraq and Syria. After them came the Babylonians.

BABYLON AND ISRAEL

The next great world power was headquartered in the ancient city of Babylon in what is now southern Iraq. Babylon eliminated the Assyrian kingdom from the face of the earth in 610 BC.[3] And though the Egyptian empire hung around as a great empire, it was an empire in decline. Babylon was the "big daddy" from 610 BC to 539 BC. The great ruler of Babylon was a man by the name of Nebuchadnezzar, whom Saddam Hussein idolized. He had a unique history with Israel. He conquered Jerusalem in 597 BC and began to deport many Jews to Babylon (2 Kings 24:10–12). For a time he allowed Jewish kings to reign under his author-ity in Jerusalem, but in 587, after numerous rebellions, Nebuchadnezzar leveled the capital of Jerusalem. This included the great temple built by Solomon about four hundred years earlier (2 Kings 25). Then he took many of the conquered Jews back to Babylon to serve as slaves in what is known as the Babylonian captivity. This was an especially dark period of Jewish history. Babylon and Nebuchadnezzar would become synony-mous with worldly power opposed to God and godly values. They would both face the judgment of God. In this light, they both play a huge role in biblical history with Israel that cannot be overlooked. What is that?

God will use worldly pagan nations to bring judgment on His rebellious people. The book of Judges deals with this scenario over and over. Israel falls away from God through idol worship and debauchery, God sends pagan enemy nations to bring judgment on them until they cry out to God to have mercy on them, and He raises up a temporary savior (or judge) to lead Israel to repentance and then overthrow their oppressors.

This is what God did through Nebuchadnezzar and Babylon. The prophet of Israel most associated with pleading with Israel to repent was Jeremiah. He made it clear that if they did not, God would send Nebuchadnezzar and Babylon to bring His judgment upon them. "Thus says the LORD, 'Behold, a people is coming from the north land, / And a great nation will be aroused from the remote parts of the earth'" (Jeremiah 6:22). The enemy from the north was Babylon. They were a powerful and cruel conqueror. From a human perspective they were unstoppable. From the theological perspective of Jeremiah, they represented the wrath and judgment of God on rebellious Israel.

> And the LORD has sent to you all His servants the prophets again and again, but you have not listened nor inclined your ear to hear, saying, "Turn now everyone from his evil way and from the evil of your deeds, and dwell on the land which the LORD has given to you and your fore-fathers forever and ever; and do not go after other gods to serve them and to worship them, and do not provoke Me to anger with the work of your hands, and I will do you no harm."
>
> "Yet you have not listened to Me," declares the LORD, "in order that you might provoke Me to anger with the work of your hands to your own harm. Therefore thus says the LORD of hosts, 'Because you have not obeyed My words, behold, I will send and take all the families of the north,' declares the LORD, 'and I will send to Nebuchadnezzar king of Babylon, My servant, and will bring them against this land and against its inhabitants and against all these nations round about;

and I will utterly destroy them and make them a horror and a hissing, and an everlasting desolation. Moreover, I will take from them the voice of joy and the voice of gladness, the voice of the bridegroom and the voice of the bride, the sound of the millstones and the light of the lamp. This whole land will be a desolation and a horror, and these nations will serve the king of Babylon seventy years.'" (Jeremiah 25:4–11)

That judgment day came between 597 and 587 BC.

One of God's prophets who was taken to Babylon in the Babylonian captivity was Daniel. And with him were also three young heroes of the faith. Daniel 1:6 tells us their names were Hananiah, Mishael, and Azariah. Biblical Jews and Christians know them by their Babylonian names, Shadrach, Meshach, and Abed-nego. In Daniel 3, they show the ultimate example of faith when they are given the choice by Nebuchadnezzar to bow down to the great golden image of Nebuchadnezzar that was ninety feet high or be thrown into the fiery furnace. Their response in Daniel 3:16–18 is classic: "Shadrach, Meshach and Abed-nego replied to the king, 'O Nebuchadnezzar, we do not need to give you an answer concerning this matter. If it be so, our God whom we serve is able to deliver us from the furnace of blazing fire; and He will deliver us out of your hand, O king. But even if He does not, let it be known to you, O king, that we are not going to serve your gods or worship the golden image that you have set up.'"

Nebuchadnezzar was furious because he was a classic megalomaniac ruler. But more than that, he is truly an anti-Christ type figure who egocentrically wanted to unify the world around himself. Shadrach, Meshach, and Abed-nego showed that real faith believes God is all-powerful. He can do anything. He could miraculously intervene to save them from the fiery furnace, but even if He did not—they would choose to trust and obey Him. What faith! What incredible faith! God did miraculously save them and prove that He is all-powerful even over the world's greatest powers, Nebuchadnezzar and Babylon. But that is not all.

God used Daniel to interpret Nebuchadnezzar's dreams, revealing the astounding prophecy that after Babylon, the Medo-Persian Empire would arise as the dominant world power, followed by the Greeks then the Romans. He reveals this in Daniel 2. But Nebuchadnezzar didn't tell his sorcerers and magicians or even Daniel the dream he had. He told them to tell him what he dreamed and give him the right interpretation of the dream. By the power of God, Daniel was able to do so, and he was able to have a powerful witness to Nebuchadnezzar of the one and only true God. Then Nebuchadnezzar made Daniel, a foreigner, a Hebrew slave, the prime minister over the Babylonian kingdom, answerable only to Nebuchadnezzar—as Joseph was years earlier with the pharaoh of Egypt (Daniel 2:46–49).

Nebuchadnezzar was so impressed with the wisdom and faith of Daniel, and later with Shadrach, Meshach and Abed-nego, that he began to profess faith in their God as the one true God in Daniel 4. Then Nebuchadnezzar had another dream, a disturbing dream. Again, Daniel correctly interpreted it, though it terrified him to do so, He told the king he would be struck insane and live with animals in the fields and act like an animal. This happened in Daniel 4:28–33:

> All this happened to Nebuchadnezzar the king. Twelve months later he was walking on the roof of the royal palace of Babylon. The king reflected and said, "Is this not Babylon the great, which I myself have built as a royal residence by the might of my power and for the glory of my majesty?" While the word was in the king's mouth, a voice came from heaven, saying, "King Nebuchadnezzar, to you it is declared: sovereignty has been removed from you, and you will be driven away from mankind, and your dwelling place will be with the beasts of the field. You will be given grass to eat like cattle, and seven periods of time will pass over you until you recognize that the Most High is ruler over the realm of mankind and bestows it on whomever He wishes." Immediately the word concerning Nebuchadnezzar was fulfilled; and he was driven away from mankind and began eating grass like cattle, and his body was

drenched with the dew of heaven until his hair had grown like eagles' feathers and his nails like birds' claws.

Nebuchadnezzar became filled with pride. He felt his greatness was all because of himself. God humbled him to remind him and all people like him that his greatness came from God. After seven years, when Nebuchadnezzar repented, reason and rule and majesty returned to him.

> But at the end of that period, I, Nebuchadnezzar, raised my eyes toward heaven and my reason returned to me, and I blessed the Most High and praised and honored Him who lives forever;
>
> > *For His dominion is an everlasting dominion,*
> > *And His kingdom endures from generation to generation.*
> > *All the inhabitants of the earth are accounted as nothing,*
> > *But He does according to His will in the host of heaven*
> > *And among the inhabitants of earth;*
> > *And no one can ward off His hand*
> > *Or say to Him, "What have You done?"*
>
> At that time my reason returned to me. And my majesty and splendor were restored to me for the glory of my kingdom, and my counselors and my nobles began seeking me out; so I was reestablished in my sovereignty, and surpassing greatness was added to me.
>
> Now I, Nebuchadnezzar, praise, exalt and honor the King of heaven, for all His works are true and His ways just, and He is able to humble those who walk in pride. (Daniel 4:34–37)

What happened to Nebuchadnezzar is a reminder of what can happen to anyone puffed up with pride. God will humble us and remind us that He is God and we are not.

Daniel outlived the king and continued to serve Nebuchadnezzar's successor, Belshazzar. He also interpreted his dreams and courageously prophesied that he would be overthrown by the Medo-Persian Empire:

"Now this is the inscription that was written out: 'MENE, MENE, TEKEL, UPHARSIN.' This is the interpretation of the message: 'MENE'—God has numbered your kingdom and put an end to it. 'TEKEL'—you have been weighed on the scales and found deficient. 'PERES'—your kingdom has been divided and given over to the Medes and Persians." Then Belshazzar gave orders, and they clothed Daniel with purple and put a necklace of gold around his neck, and issued a proclamation concerning him that he now had authority as the third ruler in the kingdom. That same night Belshazzar the Chaldean king was slain. (Daniel 5:25–30)

Daniel's prophecy came true, and he went on to serve another king of another kingdom and even survive a lion's den to do so.

THE RESTORATION OF ISRAEL

God was making it clear that He will use worldly pagan power to discipline and bring judgment on His people. He does this in hopes that His chosen people will repent and turn again to Him in faith. But God is also clear; those He uses to judge Israel will face the wrath of God for their worldly evil, cruelty, and pride. Nebuchadnezzar and the Babylonians were the greatest worldly power of their day. Though they were feared by all, they had no power over God, who was orchestrating events to teach Israel and all of us who trust Scripture as God's Word that God is in charge of history. Israel would be restored. God had not forgotten them. The same prophet who irritated Israel to no end with his gloom-and-doom prophecy was the same one who would speak God's word concerning Israel's restoration. Jeremiah's prophecy in Jeremiah 29:4–14 speaks of this.

"Thus says the LORD of hosts, the God of Israel, to all the exiles whom I have sent into exile from Jerusalem to Babylon, 'Build houses and live in them; and plant gardens and eat their produce. Take wives and become the fathers of sons and daughters, and take wives for your sons and give your daughters to husbands, that they may bear sons and daughters; and multiply there and do not decrease. Seek the welfare of the city where I have sent you into exile, and pray to the LORD on its behalf; for in its welfare you will have welfare.'

"For thus says the LORD of hosts, the God of Israel, 'Do not let your prophets who are in your midst and your diviners deceive you, and do not listen to the dreams which they dream. For they prophesy falsely to you in My name; I have not sent them,' declares the LORD.

"For thus says the LORD, 'When seventy years have been completed for Babylon, I will visit you and fulfill My good word to you, to bring you back to this place. For I know the plans that I have for you,' declares the LORD, 'plans for welfare and not for calamity to give you a future and a hope. Then you will call upon Me and come and pray to Me, and I will listen to you. You will seek Me and find Me when you search for Me with all your heart. I will be found by you,' declares the LORD, 'and I will restore your fortunes and will gather you from all the nations and from all the places where I have driven you,' declares the LORD, 'and I will bring you back to the place from where I sent you into exile.'"

Verse 11 has become a key theme verse to many Christians—especially Christians facing difficult times: "'For I know the plans that I have for you,' declares the LORD, 'plans for welfare and not for calamity to give you a future and a hope.'" It is a wonderful promise of God to all His followers that He is in charge of the plans for our life. No matter how difficult life becomes, God has not forgotten us. We still have reason to be hopeful about the future.

Understanding the promise of God in Jeremiah 29:11 has even deeper meaning when we know the context in which it was said. Earlier, Jeremiah had hard words for the people of Israel. His prophecy of God's judgment on His chosen people through a pagan power like Babylon was not a popular, people-pleasing message. He and his message were rejected by a rebellious people who didn't want to hear the truth. Israel, then, was like so many Christians today who are described in 2 Timothy 4:3–4: "For the time will come when they will not endure sound doctrine; but wanting to have their ears tickled, they will accumulate for themselves teachers in accordance to their own desires, and will turn away their ears from the truth and will turn aside to myths."

Yet as hard as Jeremiah's word from God was, it was still seasoned with God's grace. Yes, God is unhappy with you. Yes, He must bring discipline and judgment on you, but He has not given up on you. He still has great plans for you—a future and a hope. "Then [this key word means 'when'] you will call upon Me and come and pray to Me, and I will listen to you" (Jeremiah 29:12). Then God assured Israel that He would restore her blessings and gather her from all the nations from which she had been driven. "'You will seek Me and find Me when you search for Me with all your heart. I will be found by you,' declares the LORD, 'and I will restore your fortunes and will gather you from all the nations and from all the places where I have driven you,' declares the LORD, 'and I will bring you back to the place from where I sent you into exile'" (vv.13–14).

What did Jeremiah mean by God saying, "I will gather you from *all the nations* and all the places I have driven you"? Biblical prophecy often has layers of meaning. It is God's Word through the prophet speaking to the contemporary events of that day. Because it is the Word of God and God is over all history and time, His Word speaks to a specific time in history, like the Babylonian captivity of Israel. Yet God's Word speaks universally in verses such as Jeremiah 29:11 and of more than one event in Jeremiah 29:14. At this point in history Israel had been driven to Babylon, but about six hundred years later in AD 70, Rome leveled Jerusalem and the Jewish temple.

Over the next sixty years they began to drive the Jews from their land to nations all around the world. Little did many Jews and the world know that almost two thousand years later the words of God in Jeremiah 29:14 would be fulfilled once again. At this very hour, the ingathering of Jews from all over the world continues to take place in Israel. It began en masse after 1948 when Israel was reborn as a nation in the land God promised them all the way back to Abraham, Isaac, and Jacob.

What is so interesting about Saddam Hussein wanting to restore Iraq to greatness like the days of Nebuchadnezzar and Babylon is his effort was futile. They both mistreated Israel, but Israel will not be destroyed. Even when Israel was taken into Babylonian captivity and seemed to be no more, she didn't disappear. She will not be destroyed. Israel is God's chosen people.

After the Babylonian captivity Israel returned home. Later in AD 70 Rome leveled Jerusalem and expelled the Jews from Israel and Judea to never return again. Yet even after almost two thousand years, Israel was born again as a nation, and Hebrew—the language that was used only by rabbis and at bar mitzvahs—was restored.

At least once more in history, things will look bleak for Israel as the final Antichrist rules over modern-day Babylon, described in Revelation 17–18. It is a symbolic Babylon that represents worldly might and values. But Israel will survive even that, as we'll see. It's the promise of God's Word.

8

ISRAEL'S GREATEST THREAT TODAY
Iran

*Thus says Cyrus king of Persia, "The LORD, the God of heaven, has given me
all the kingdoms of the earth and He has appointed me to build Him a house in
Jerusalem, which is in Judah. Whoever there is among you of all His people, may
his God be with him! Let him go up to Jerusalem which is in Judah and rebuild
the house of the LORD, the God of Israel; He is the God who is in Jerusalem."*

—EZRA 1:2–3

"I srael is a disgraceful blot that should be wiped off the face of the
earth."[1] Those words were the words of Mahmoud Ahmadinejad,
the president of Iran, on October 26, 2005. This quote shocked
the Western world, and he was soundly condemned by the US, Britain,
France, Germany, and Israel. Many thought, *This man must be crazy*. Yet
this reaction reveals an epidemic of historical and biblical illiteracy.

In chapter 7, we saw the historical relationship of Israel with other
nations of the Middle East. There is one more relationship with Israel
that must be looked at—her relationship with Iran. No nation is a greater

threat to Israel and peace in the Middle East than Iran. It is a relationship that goes back thousands of years.

Regional Threats to Israel

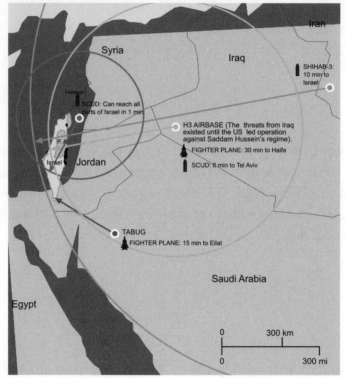

Iran is the modern-day name for the ancient kingdom of Persia. Three things must be noted about the Persian people. First of all, Persians have a rich cultural heritage. They were extremely influential in the development of civilization. Their influence was especially great in the areas of law, government, and economics. They were committed to the rule of law, and even though their kings had great power, they gave authority and support to local law. Their government became one of the best organized in the history of man. The Persian Empire was vast—from India to North Africa, from Macedonia to Asia Minor to southern Russia. The empire was divided into satraps (like nations) and those satraps into provinces (sort of like our states). Western culture tends to idolize Greco-Roman culture as the cradle of civilization, but Greece and Rome were largely influenced by Persia. The Persians developed minted coins and a money economy and vast roads to unify the empire.[2] To this day, when a Westerner is able to see behind the curtain of the oppressive Islamic regime in power, he is often surprised to find such a cultured and sophisticated people.

Second, it is important to note that Iranians are not Arabic. Most Americans lump Iranians into that group of Middle Eastern Muslim Arabs. They are Muslim, yes, but they are not Arabic. They are Persian. When Iraq and Iran engaged in a brutal war in the 1980s, it was not just Iraq versus Iran, but Arabs versus Persians. Their conflict goes back over thousands of years but reached a climax when Persia overthrew Babylon as the dominant world power in 539 BC under the leadership of Cyrus the Great.

And finally, Persia's relationship with Israel started out very well. How did this happen? From the beginning, Iran's relationship with Israel was liberating. Remember, in the Babylonian Empire, Jerusalem and the temple were destroyed and most of the Jews were taken into captivity in Babylon. When Cyrus the Great overthrew Babylon, he made the decision to let the Jews return to their homeland. The books of 2 Chronicles and Ezra tell about this:

> Now in the first year of Cyrus king of Persia—in order to fulfill the word of the LORD by the mouth of Jeremiah—the LORD stirred up the spirit of Cyrus king of Persia, so that he sent a proclamation throughout his kingdom, and also put it in writing, saying, "Thus says Cyrus king of Persia, 'The LORD, the God of heaven, has given me all the kingdoms of the earth, and He has appointed me to build Him a house in Jerusalem, which is in Judah. Whoever there is among you of all His people, may the LORD his God be with him, and let him go up!'" (2 Chronicles 36:22–23)

Those words are repeated almost verbatim in Ezra 1:1–3. This was a great beginning to the relationship between Persia and Israel.

THE AMAZING PROPHECY OF CYRUS

In our last chapter we looked at the prophecy of Jeremiah to Israel that God would send Babylon to bring judgment on Israel and they would serve Babylon. God used another prophet who lived about two hundred years before Cyrus the Great to share even more specific insight.

> "It is I who says of Cyrus, 'He is My shepherd!
>   And he will perform all My desire.'
>   And he declares of Jerusalem, 'She will be built,'
>   And of the temple, 'Your foundation will be laid.'"

> Thus says the Lord to Cyrus His anointed,
>   Whom I have taken by the right hand,
>   To subdue nations before him
>   And to loose the loins of kings;
>   To open doors before him so that gates will not be shut:
> "I will go before you and make the rough places smooth;
>   I will shatter the doors of bronze and cut through their iron bars.
> I will give you the treasures of darkness
>   And hidden wealth of secret places,
>   So that you may know that it is I,
>   The Lord, the God of Israel, who calls you by your name.
> For the sake of Jacob My servant,
>   And Israel My chosen one,
>   I have also called you by your name;
>   I have given you a title of honor
>   Though you have not known Me.
> I am the Lord, and there is no other;

Besides Me there is no God.

I will gird you, though you have not known Me;

That men may know from the rising to the setting of the sun

That there is no one besides Me.

I am the LORD, and there is no other." (Isaiah 44:28–45:6)

This is phenomenal. Long before Cyrus even existed, long before the Babylonian and Persian empires were dominant, God led Isaiah to prophesy these exact events of history. What is equally remarkable is that when Cyrus conquered Babylon, Jewish leaders went to him and showed him this passage in God's Holy Word.[3]

Can you imagine how this impacted him concerning the God of the Jews? Cyrus had already shown worldly wisdom by publicly honoring the gods of each nation and people group he conquered. This was part of his political genius that matched his military genius of uniting his empire while respecting each nation's beliefs and traditions.[4] Historical documents concerning Cyrus were discovered in the ruins of Babylon in the nineteenth century. They said, "I am Cyrus, the king of the world . . . Marduk, a great god, rejoices at my pious deeds." Yet Paul Johnson, the great British historian, wrote, "Cyrus himself was a Zoroastrian, believing in one eternal, beneficent being, 'creator of all things through the holy spirit.'"[5] This ancient religion of Zoroastrianism was developed in Persia between 1400–1000 BC. It permeated Persian thought. Zoroastrianism teaches that there is one God over all.[6]

What a eureka moment for Cyrus to hear Jewish leaders reading from their Holy Book the words of the prophet Isaiah written long before Babylon was dominant and long before he even existed. What a moment of destiny that had to be. This was clear instruction from God not only that Jerusalem should be rebuilt and the foundation of the temple laid, but that Cyrus was the man God had chosen to do it. God was blessing him with great success so that Cyrus might know the one true God of Israel. How awesome is the trustworthiness of God's Word. What an amazing reminder that God is over all of history.

The book of Ezra describes how this calling of Cyrus unfolded. The prophet wrote of Cyrus's commands to return articles of the temple that Nebuchadnezzar had plundered (1:5–11). This represented enormous wealth that Cyrus was releasing to Israel because he believed the Word of God concerning his destiny. Israelites began to return in great numbers, and the temple began to be restored (Ezra 3).

The work would take years, and when the returning exiles began to face opposition, the Jewish leaders sent a letter to one of Cyrus's successors, requesting help. To the Jews' dismay, he ordered the rebuilding work in Jerusalem to stop. Interestingly, the opposition came from Samaritans (Jewish half-breeds who had intermarried with Assyrians), Edomites (heirs of Esau), and Arabs (heirs of Ishmael). But then years later another one of his successors, Darius the Great, checked the historical records and found Cyrus's edict for the rebuilding the temple in Jerusalem and ordered the work to continue (Ezra 5–6). The temple was finally completed in 516 BC under Darius's reign, four years after he ordered work to continue.

About eighty years later, another Persian king named Artaxerxes allowed the brilliant leader Nehemiah to leave his court and rebuild the wall around Jerusalem. Obviously, the Persian Empire blessed the Jews in many ways.

TENSIONS BETWEEN PERSIA AND ISRAEL

The unique leadership of Cyrus and Darius set the tone for Persia's relationship with Israel. Even though that relationship began well, all did not continue smoothly. Daniel had risen to great power in the Babylonian government. After the Medo-Persian Empire conquered Babylon, the prophet continued to be a respected government leader in that region. But the jealousy of government officials over a foreigner with so much power caused them to plot against Daniel. Daniel 6 is an incredible story of God's protection of Daniel, thrown into a den of lions. When Daniel survived the night, it caused King Darius to proclaim Daniel's God as the one true God:

> Then the king arose at dawn, at the break of day, and went in haste to the lions' den. When he had come near the den to Daniel, he cried out with a troubled voice. The king spoke and said to Daniel, "Daniel, servant of the living God, has your God, whom you constantly serve, been able to deliver you from the lions?"
>
> Then Daniel spoke to the king, "O king, live forever! My God sent His angel and shut the lions' mouths and they have not harmed me, inasmuch as I was found innocent before Him; and also toward you, O king, I have committed no crime."
>
> Then the king was very pleased and gave orders for Daniel to be taken up out of the den. So Daniel was taken up out of the den and no injury whatever was found on him, because he had trusted in his God. The king then gave orders, and they brought those men who had maliciously accused Daniel, and they cast them, their children and their wives into the lions' den; and they had not reached the bottom of the den before the lions overpowered them and crushed all their bones.
>
> Then Darius the king wrote to all the peoples, nations and men of every language who were living in all the land: "May your peace abound! I make a decree that in all the dominion of my kingdom men are to fear and tremble before the God of Daniel;
>> For He is the living God and enduring forever,
>> And His kingdom is one which will not be destroyed,
>> And His dominion will be forever.
> He delivers and rescues and performs signs and wonders
>> In heaven and on earth,
>> Who has also delivered Daniel from the power of the lions."
>
> So this Daniel enjoyed success in the reign of Darius and in the reign of Cyrus the Persian. (Daniel 6:19–28)

Just as God had done with Daniel in his faithful witness to the Babylonian tyrant Nebuchadnezzar, now He did with the king of the

Persian Empire. No matter who is king, God is in charge. God is over all.

But the Persian Empire continued to expand, and serious trouble arose for the Jews. It happened under one of the weaker Persian kings, Ahasuerus, also known in history as King Xerxes. King Ahasuerus had ditched his first queen, and plans were made for him to choose a new queen from a national beauty pageant comprised of beautiful young virgins from all over the empire.

The king chose a beautiful young virgin named Esther. What the Persian king did not know was that Esther was a Jew. Her story is described in the book of Esther, and even though the name of God is not mentioned in the entire book, His providential hand is clearly orchestrating all the unfolding drama. What a dramatic story it is.

King Ahasuerus promoted an egotistical and ambitious man to be prime minister over his entire kingdom. He was a classic "little man." I don't mean little in stature (he may have been), but a little man in a big role of power. Haman was his name, and Haman was all about Haman. Haman enjoyed the Persian custom of people bowing down to him whenever he entered the king's gate. Yet he was furious that one man, named Mordecai, refused to bow. Haman did not know that Mordecai was a close relative of Queen Esther. He was her cousin who raised her. As a matter of fact, shortly after Esther was selected as queen, Mordecai had overheard a plot to assassinate the king and told Esther, who in turn told the king, and the guilty parties were both executed. What Mordecai had done to save the king was recorded in the king's records.

Haman didn't know any of that. He was just in a snit that Mordecai refused to bow to him. When he inquired why he did not, he was told it was because Mordecai was a Jew. Jews only bow to God. So in a classic example of overkill, Haman devised a plot to exterminate all the Jews in Persia. He presented an edict to the king with the implication that these people were troublemakers who refused to obey all the king's laws.

Rather than inquire who this was and ask for more details, the lazy and careless King Ahasuerus signed the edict that called for the extermination of all the Jews. For years, anyone who read this story in Esther thought of Adolf Hitler and his "Final Solution to the Jewish Question." Certainly no idea has been straighter from the pits of hell than Hitler's plan that resulted in the Holocaust of almost 6 million Jews. Yet Haman's plan was just the same. Obviously it came from the same source—for one character trait of the devil is that he hates those whom God loves. And God loves the Jewish people in a specially chosen way. So all through history, evil men and women have been seduced by the devil in blaming Jews for hundreds of irrational reasons.

But from the standpoint of history, even though Haman had a devil-filled heart like Hitler, he would really be more like the president of Iran, Mahmoud Ahmadinejad. Both are Persian rulers. Both answer to just one man—Haman to the king and Ahmadinejad to the great Imam of Iran. Both are little men filled with anti-Semitic hatred. Both irrationally blame the Jews with outrageous slander and lies. And both will have been proven unsuccessful in fulfilling their demonic plans.

When Mordecai informed Esther of Haman's plot and the king's approval, she was horrified. But when Mordecai urged her to intercede before the king, she did not want to do so; she knew to approach the king without being summoned could mean death. Yet Mordecai was determined and sent this message to Esther: "Do not imagine that you in the king's palace can escape any more than all the Jews. For if you remain silent at this time, relief and deliverance will arise for the Jews from another place and you and your father's house will perish. And who knows whether you have not attained royalty *for such a time as this*?" (Esther 4:13–14; emphasis added).

What a statement of faith. What a courageous challenge. What a sense of destiny. Mordecai's words to Esther are words for all believers when we don't want to get involved in problems of this world, when we don't want to rock the boat, when we don't want to risk status and wealth and position to do the right thing. What a call to action. What a call to courageous faith.

With this, Esther responded to the call with quiet, prayerful courage: "Go, assemble all the Jews who are found in Susa, and fast for me; do not eat or drink for three days, night or day. I and my maidens also will fast in the same way. And thus I will go in to the king, which is not according to the law; and if I perish, I perish" (Esther 4:16). What an inspiration. What an example of their faith. Esther is an example for us all.

While this was taking place, Haman had ordered gallows built so all could see where he planned to hang Mordecai. But as God clearly orchestrated the drama, the tables were turned through Esther's intervention with the king. Mordecai was honored, Haman was hanged, and the Jews of Persia were saved. Once again I urge you to put down this book and read this dramatic story in the book of Esther. No director on Broadway can direct a drama as God can.

Ahmadinejad's day is coming, just as Haman's did. How God orchestrates events, only God knows. But God is in charge of the plans of history, and the promise God made to Abraham years ago is still a promise today. "I will bless those who bless you, and I will curse those who curse you." Yes. Ahmadinejad and Iran are a great threat to this world. They are a great threat to Israel. But Israel will not be permanently destroyed. She may suffer greatly and unjustly—but she will not be destroyed. God will have the final say. Haman learned this. Ahmadinejad will as well.

PART TWO

CONFLICTING
PERSPECTIVES

9

THE JEWISH PERSPECTIVE

Then you shall be My own possession among all the peoples, for all the earth is Mine; and you shall be to Me a kingdom of priests and a holy nation.

—EXODUS 19:5–6

As we have seen, three of the world's most influential religions dominate the Middle East: Judaism, Christianity, and Islam. Judaism began with Abraham and flows through Isaac and Jacob, who was renamed Israel. From Jacob (Israel) came twelve sons, the origin of the twelve tribes of Israel. From the twelve tribes of Israel came the founding of the ancient nation of Israel under Moses with the Mosaic Law (although the odyssey of slavery in Egypt for about four hundred years delayed the formal beginning of Israel under Moses). Then came the claiming of the land under Joshua.

Eventually, God reluctantly gave Israel the right to have kings like other nations. The first three are the most famous: Saul, who looked like a king but was one sorry leader; David, the greatest and most loved of all the Hebrew kings, whose passion was both his greatest strength in his relationship with God and his greatest weakness in lustful adultery with Bathsheba; and Solomon, David's son, who was blessed with unparalleled wisdom and administrative leadership but who did not finish strong. After these three giants on the historical landscape of Judaism, there were many kings and many prophets up until about four hundred years before the birth of Christ.

All of this is recorded in the Jewish Bible that Christians call the Old Testament. In part 1, we studied some of the most prominent stories of the Old Testament. Judaism also has sacred writings that supplement Scripture, called the Apocrypha. Though these books are found in the Catholic Bible between the Old and New Testaments, they are not considered Holy Scripture by the Jewish people.[1] Ever since King David proclaimed Jerusalem as the capital city of Israel, Jerusalem has represented the heart and soul of Judaism. Years earlier, it was the site of Abraham's willingness to sacrifice Isaac. Years later, it would be the site of the first temple, built by Solomon and then destroyed by Nebuchadnezzar of Babylon in 587 BC. The second temple was rebuilt in Jerusalem under Persian rule and later updated under King Herod, who ruled during Jesus' birth. Then it was destroyed by the Romans in AD 70 and has never been rebuilt. Today the Dome of the Rock of Islam sits on that ancient site.

THE JEWISH PERSPECTIVE
FROM A CHRISTIAN STANDPOINT

I must qualify my insights on the Jewish perspective. I'm a follower of Jesus Christ. He is my Lord and Savior, and I believe He is the long-awaited Messiah of the Jews. It is impossible for me as a Christian to give an unbiased account of the Jewish perspective. But I would like to start from the standpoint of one of the most common questions I hear from people both inside and outside the church: "Bryant, how do you explain that the Jews are God's chosen people, yet they have rejected Jesus as their Messiah?"

Years ago I preached a sermon series called "The Jewish People and Christianity" from Romans 9–11 that focused on this question. The first message of the series was entitled "The Jewish Question." Oh my, what a terrible mistake I made. For today's Jews, "the Jewish question" means one thing—a reference to Hitler's Holocaust, which he labeled "the Final Solution to the Jewish Question."

From the moment the title appeared on the marquee in front of the church, our office received angry phone calls and e-mails. I was absolutely sick that I had unintentionally offended Jewish people in the community, especially since I have such a love for the Jews and Israel. As a pastor who loves history, I was sick that I had been so historically ignorant. I made a very heartfelt apology to the Jewish community in North Atlanta and changed the title of the message to "A Passionate Love for the Jews." The text was the same, Romans 9:1–5. This passage describes Christ's love for the Jews, Paul's love for the Jews, and it allowed me to share my testimony of my special love for the Jewish people and for Israel.

With that in mind, let's look at the Jewish perspective from a Christian viewpoint. This is even more complicated when I approach this topic from a biblical perspective, for many Jews in America and Israel are not biblical Jews. Many of today's Jews don't describe themselves as religious. In Israel, many call themselves Zionist but not religious, meaning their focus is more on the land than on God. They are Jewish in ethnicity and may honor rituals and holidays that have religious meaning as part of their Jewish heritage and tradition, while not calling themselves religious. So to write of the Jewish perspective, most of my focus will be on the biblical Jewish perspective more than Jewish ethnicity and tradition.

To do that, I can think of no better source than the apostle Paul. Before he came to faith in Christ, Paul testified, "I am a Jew, born in Tarsus of Cilicia, but brought up in this city, educated under Gamaliel, strictly according to the law of our fathers, being zealous for God just as you all are today" (Acts 22:3). Gamaliel was the premier rabbi of Paul's day. So he was taught by the best. He went on to write in Galatians 1:14, "And I was advancing in Judaism beyond many of my contemporaries among my countrymen, being more extremely zealous for my ancestral traditions." This is why Paul so vigorously persecuted Christians. He knew what followers of Christ believed was contrary to traditional Judaism, and he was appalled by it. He was a classic heresy hunter who felt this misguided movement among his fellow Jews must be stopped.

THE CHOSEN PEOPLE

So what does Paul reveal to us about the Jewish perspective? He best summarized it in Romans 9:3–5: "My kinsmen according to the flesh . . . are Israelites, to whom belongs the adoption as sons, and the glory and the covenants and the giving of the Law and the temple service and the promises, whose are the fathers, and from whom is the Christ according to the flesh, who is over all, God blessed forever. Amen."

They Are Israelites

God chose Jacob to be the heir of the covenant commitment He made with Abraham. Eventually, God changed Jacob's name to Israel. All of this occurred because of God's grace—not from anything Abraham or Isaac or Jacob deserved. As a matter of fact, they did not. None of us deserves God's favor; it is all by God's grace.

They Are Adopted as Sons

Jews have been specially chosen to be the adopted children of God. This is where the phrase "children of Israel" comes from. God made this very clear to Moses when He called him to return to Egypt at eighty years of age to confront the most powerful man in the world, Pharaoh. And God called Moses not only to confront Pharaoh but to command him to voluntarily release his slave labor force of about 2 million Jews, who brought enormous wealth to Egypt with all that free labor. God told Moses to tell him, "Thus says the LORD, 'Israel is My son, My firstborn, so I said to you, "Let My son go that he may serve Me""" (Exodus 4:22–23).

Paul also knew that in Mosaic Law this adoption as children of God was clearly taught: "You are the sons of the LORD your God . . . For you are a holy people to the LORD your God, and the LORD has chosen you to be a people for His own possession out of all the peoples who are on the face of the earth" (Deuteronomy 14:1–2). Biblical Jews clearly understand that by the grace of God, He chose them to be His children out of all the people groups on earth. What an awesome privilege!

Wise parents of adopted children make it clear to those children how special they are. They say, "Out of all the children in this world, your mom and dad have chosen you to be our very own." In this light, there is no greater honor than being an adopted child of God.

They Experienced God's Glory

Because Israelites have been especially chosen, God has revealed to them His glory in extraordinary ways. He supernaturally empowered Abraham and Sarah to have God's covenant child, Isaac, at 100 and 90 years of age, respectively. He appeared to Moses in the burning bush to call him to lead the children of Israel to freedom (Exodus 3). He gave Moses the Law of God on Mount Sinai (Exodus 20). His glory came upon the tabernacle of God: "Then the cloud covered the tent of meeting, and *the glory of the LORD filled the tabernacle*. Moses was not able to enter the tent of meeting because the cloud had settled on it, and *the glory of the LORD filled the tabernacle*" (Exodus 40:34–35; emphasis added).

God also anointed the Hebrew prophets with the Word of God for their age with words of God that are timeless and speak to everyone in every age. His glory is truly seen in the timeless power of His Word.

They Were Given Covenants

God made His initial covenant with Abraham in Genesis 12:1–3:

> Now the LORD said to Abram,
>> "Go forth from your country,
>> And from your relatives
>> And from your father's house,
>> To the land which I will show you;
>> And I will make you a great nation,

And I will bless you,

And make your name great;

And so you shall be a blessing;

And I will bless those who bless you,

And the one who curses you I will curse.

And in you all the families of the earth will be blessed."

The covenant included God's promise of the land to the heirs of Abraham: "To your descendants I will give this land" (Genesis 12:7). He reiterated that promise in Genesis 17:8: "I will give to you and to your descendants after you, the land of your sojournings, all the land of Canaan, for an everlasting possession; and I will be their God."

God would build a great nation from Abraham's seed. This was repeated to Abraham in Genesis 15:5: "And He took him outside and said, 'Now look toward the heavens, and count the stars, if you are able to count them.' And He said to him, 'So shall your descendants be.'" God reiterated this promise to Abraham again in Genesis 17:1–8: "I will establish My covenant between Me and you and your descendants after you throughout their generations *for an everlasting covenant,* to be God to you and to your descendants after you" (v. 7; emphasis added).

God made it clear these are "everlasting covenants" concerning the promised land and being God's chosen people. In other words, they are not conditional on how Israel responds or lives. God later reiterated these covenants with Abraham's grandson, Jacob, when He changed his name to Israel in Genesis 35:10–12:

God said to him,

"Your name is Jacob;

You shall no longer be called Jacob,

But Israel shall be your name."

Thus He called him Israel.

God also said to him,

"I am God Almighty;

Be fruitful and multiply;

A nation and a company of nations shall come from you,

And kings shall come forth from you.

The land which I gave to Abraham and Isaac,

I will give it to you,

And I will give the land to your descendants after you."

Obviously, God made His will clear to the patriarchs of Israel.

God promised to bless Abraham and his heirs. He would make the name of Abraham great. And oh, how it is to this day! He is the father of Judaism, Christianity, and Islam. But He would also lead the Jewish people to be a blessing to the nations of the world. How can you explain the enormous contribution the Jewish people have been to this world? From the Law of Moses in the Ten Commandments that contributes to the essence of civilization to the number of Nobel prize winners over the last hundred years, their contribution to humanity as well as science, the arts, and business is extraordinary. Do you realize that since the Nobel prize began just over a hundred years ago, Jewish people (who make up just .02 percent of the world's population) have received a fourth of the Nobel prizes awarded in the sciences? By comparison, Muslims (who make up 25 percent of the world's population) have won only a handful.[2] It is phenomenal what Jews have contributed to this world in spite of being the most persecuted people group in the history of man.

Where so many Jews have misunderstood God's call in being a blessing to the world is in pointing their fellow man to the one true God. It is the greatest blessing that can ever be offered.

God would bless those who bless Abraham and his heirs, the Jews, and curse those who curse them. This has a huge impact on biblical Christians' love for the Jews and support of Israel.

God also made everlasting covenants with King David concerning his throne: "When your days are complete and you lie down with your fathers, I will raise up your descendant after you, who will come forth from you, and I will establish his kingdom. He shall build a house for

My name, and I will establish the throne of his kingdom forever . . . Your house and your kingdom shall endure before Me forever; your throne shall be established forever" (2 Samuel 7:12–13, 16). Christians believe Jesus is the eternal heir to David's throne, and the world will see this when He returns.

The covenants of Israel that are *conditional* have to do with Israel's obedience to God's commands. "If you do this, then I will bless you." Exodus 19:5–6 speaks to this before God gave Israel the Ten Commandments through His servant Moses: "'Now then, if you will indeed obey My voice and keep My covenant, then you shall be My own possession among all the peoples, for all the earth is Mine; and you shall be to Me a kingdom of priests and a holy nation.' These are the words that you shall speak to the sons of Israel." Prophets like Hosea, Isaiah, Jeremiah, and Ezekiel preached this over and over: when Jews turn from God and do not obey, they lose the blessing of God and face the discipline and punishment of God.

GIVEN THE LAW

God gave Moses the bulk of His Law for the new nation of Israel in Exodus 20–24, and much of the books of Leviticus and Deuteronomy. Some of the Law deals with moral relationships between God and man. Much deals with relationships between man and man. And some of it deals with ceremonial law. The Mount Everest of the Law that is God's great gift to Israel and the world is the Ten Commandments, given in Exodus 20:3–17:

1. You shall have no other gods before Me.
2. You shall not make for yourself an idol, or any likeness of what is in heaven above or on the earth beneath or in the water under the earth.
3. You shall not take the name of the LORD your God in vain.
4. Remember the Sabbath day, to keep it holy.

5. Honor your father and your mother.
6. You shall not murder.
7. You shall not commit adultery.
8. You shall not steal.
9. You shall not bear false witness against your neighbor.
10. You shall not covet your neighbor's house; you shall not covet your neighbor's wife or his male servant or his female servant or his ox or his donkey or anything that belongs to your neighbor.

There is a huge difference that Jews and Christians have over the Law. Jews see the Law as guidelines to holy and righteous living—a way of earning God's favor. Christians see it as making us aware of how impossible it is to obey God in our own strength and thus convicting us of our need for a Savior who forgives us and transforms our hearts from within. Then through the leading of the Holy Spirit and teaching of the Word, we have an inner desire to obey God's law.

TEMPLE SERVICE

The service to the temple of God is described in Exodus 25–31, 40, and in the book of Leviticus. Hebrews 9:1–7 explains how Christianity and Christ's new covenant are different from God's old covenant when it comes to temple service and worship. The Jewish temple, originally built by Solomon on Mount Moriah in Jerusalem, is a very special site. It is where Abraham was willing to sacrifice Isaac and now is the site of the Dome of the Rock. In part 1, we saw that the temple has been built and destroyed twice. After the second destruction by Rome in AD 70, there was no longer any place for the Jews to make sacrifices to the Lord in atonement for the people's sins. This is why Orthodox Jews gather at the Western Wall at the temple mount beneath the Dome of the Rock—to pray daily for the coming of the Messiah and for the rebuilding of the temple. It was the focal point of worshipping God in Judaism.

They Were Given the Promises of God

Many of God's promises were given to the patriarchs and to Moses and Joshua, but there are hundreds more, especially in the Psalms, Proverbs, and the prophets. A few examples are:

- Psalm 19:7: "The law of the LORD is perfect, restoring the soul; / The testimony of the LORD is sure, making wise the simple."
- Psalm 23:1–3: "The LORD is my shepherd, / I shall not want. / He makes me lie down in green pastures; / He leads me beside quiet waters. / He restores my soul; / He guides me in the paths of righteousness / For His name's sake."
- Proverbs 3:5–6: "Trust in the LORD with all your heart / And do not lean on your own understanding. / In all your ways acknowledge Him, / And He will make your paths straight."
- Isaiah 11:1–2, concerning the Messiah: "Then a shoot will spring from the stem of Jesse, / And a branch from his roots will bear fruit. / The Spirit of the LORD will rest on Him, / The spirit of wisdom and understanding, / The spirit of counsel and strength, / The spirit of knowledge and the fear of the LORD."
- Daniel 2:44: "In the days of those kings the God of heaven will set up a kingdom which will never be destroyed, and that kingdom will not be left for another people; it will crush and put an end to all these kingdoms, but it will itself endure forever."

They Have the Fathers

The patriarchs of the faith are Abraham, Isaac, and Jacob. God in His grace selected Abraham to be the father of the faith. As we've seen, God promised to build a great nation through the seed of Abraham and his wife, Sarah. God miraculously gave them the long-awaited son He had promised them when Isaac was born. From Isaac came two sons— Esau and Jacob—and by God's grace He chose Jacob as the covenant heir.

JESUS THE DIVIDING LINE

The word *Christ* means "Messiah." From the Christian perspective, no higher honor has been bestowed upon Israel and the Jews than being God's chosen people to give the world Jesus. This is the eternal connection between Judaism and Christianity. If so, then why is Jesus the dividing line for Jews and Christians?

Let's consider why Jesus was and is the dividing line.

Jesus Did Not Fit Their Image of Messiah

First of all, Jesus did not live up to their image of a Messiah. The Jews in Jesus' day were looking for a religious, political, and military Messiah to lead Israel to greatness as a nation. Because they were under the occupation of Rome, they were looking for a Messiah who would free them from Roman rule. Biblically, it is easy to see why Jesus did not live up to this image. Take the prophecy of Isaiah 9:6:

> *For a child will be born to us, a son will be given to us;*
> *And the government will rest on His shoulders;*
> *And His name will be called Wonderful Counselor, Mighty God,*
> *Eternal Father, Prince of Peace.*

You may recognize these words from Handel's *Messiah*, often performed in churches at Christmas. Yet what many Christians fail to note is that only the first line speaks to Jesus' birth. After that, when God's Word speaks of the government resting on His shoulders and how great His government will be in finally bringing peace on earth, we quickly realize that Jesus did not do that in His lifetime. As Christians familiar with the teaching of Christ and the New Testament, we know the rest of this verse refers to Jesus' Second Coming. Yet the Old Testament doesn't differentiate between the Messiah's first and second comings. For Jews who do not believe in Jesus, there is no Second Coming, only the coming of the Messiah.

Yet because Old Testament prophets were proclaiming the eternal Word of God and God sees all of history (past, present, and future at once because He is over time), sometimes the word of the prophet moves from the first and second coming of the Messiah within the same verse. As our beloved Jewish tour guide used to say to us when we urged him to trust Christ as his Messiah, "Bryant, when Messiah comes, if it is for the first time, you'll owe me an apology. If it is for the second time, I'll apologize to you."

Jesus' Teaching Was Considered Blasphemy

The major reason most Jews rejected Jesus was because of blasphemy. They thought He was disrespectful of some of their man-made laws, especially in regard to the Sabbath. And yes, they were jealous, envious of His popularity and following with the people. This was especially true because He had no credentials, no formal education or training as they did. But statements of Jesus like, "Truly, truly, I say to you, before Abraham was born, I am" (John 8:58) made them think Jesus had not only lost His mind but was committing blasphemy. Then when He said things like, "I and the Father are one" (John 10:30), they were so outraged that they tried to stone Him for claiming to be equal with God.

When the Jews arrested Jesus and He stood before the Jewish ruling body and high priest, He was commanded, "'If You are the Christ, tell us.' But He said to them, 'If I tell you, you will not believe; and if I ask a question, you will not answer. But from now on THE SON OF MAN WILL BE SEATED AT THE RIGHT HAND of the power of GOD'" (Luke 22:67–69). They responded, "Are you the Son of God?" And He said to them, "Yes, I am." This absolutely put them over the edge. This was outrageous blasphemy, for the Jews are a monotheistic people. No man could claim to be God. The penalty for blasphemy was death (Leviticus 24:16).

Yet because only Rome had the authority to execute their citizens or any people they ruled, they schemed and slandered Jesus before Pilate to have Him crucified. In their eyes, this was what He deserved. In their eyes, what they were doing was upholding the true faith. He deserved to die, for

He was a horrible influence on the Jewish people. So Jesus was crucified. In so doing, they ignored and fulfilled the Old Testament prophecy of the Messiah as the suffering servant in Isaiah 52:13–53:12:

> *Behold, My servant will prosper,*
> *He will be high and lifted up and greatly exalted.*
> *Just as many were astonished at you, My people,*
> *So His appearance was marred more than any man*
> *And His form more than the sons of men.*
> *Thus He will sprinkle many nations,*
> *Kings will shut their mouths on account of Him;*
> *For what had not been told them they will see,*
> *And what they had not heard they will understand.*
> *Who has believed our message?*
> *And to whom has the arm of the LORD been revealed?*
> *For He grew up before Him like a tender shoot,*
> *And like a root out of parched ground;*
> *He has no stately form or majesty*
> *That we should look upon Him,*
> *Nor appearance that we should be attracted to Him.*
> *He was despised and forsaken of men,*
> *A man of sorrows and acquainted with grief;*
> *And like one from whom men hide their face*
> *He was despised, and we did not esteem Him.*
> *Surely our griefs He Himself bore,*
> *And our sorrows He carried;*
> *Yet we ourselves esteemed Him stricken,*
> *Smitten of God, and afflicted.*
> *But He was pierced through for our transgressions,*
> *He was crushed for our iniquities;*
> *The chastening for our well-being fell upon Him,*
> *And by His scourging we are healed.*
> *All of us like sheep have gone astray,*

Each of us has turned to his own way;
But the LORD has caused the iniquity of us all
To fall on Him.
He was oppressed and He was afflicted,
Yet He did not open His mouth;
Like a lamb that is led to slaughter,
And like a sheep that is silent before its shearers,
So He did not open His mouth.
By oppression and judgment He was taken away;
And as for His generation, who considered
That He was cut off out of the land of the living
For the transgression of my people, to whom the stroke was due?
His grave was assigned with wicked men,
Yet He was with a rich man in His death,
Because He had done no violence,
Nor was there any deceit in His mouth.
But the LORD was pleased
To crush Him, putting Him to grief;
If He would render Himself as a guilt offering,
He will see His offspring,
He will prolong His days,
And the good pleasure of the LORD will prosper in His hand.
As a result of the anguish of His soul,
He will see it and be satisfied;
By His knowledge the Righteous One,
My Servant, will justify the many,
As He will bear their iniquities.
Therefore, I will allot Him a portion with the great,
And He will divide the booty with the strong;
Because He poured out Himself to death,
And was numbered with the transgressors;
Yet He Himself bore the sin of many,
And interceded for the transgressors.

This Old Testament prophecy of the Messiah is still largely ignored by Jews with regard to Jesus today.

Yet when Jesus died, He did not stay dead. Jewish religious leaders convinced Pilate to put a Roman guard at the tomb where Jesus was buried for fear that His disciples would steal His body and say He did what He said He would do—rise from the dead. But even that plan ran into problems. The Roman soldiers guarding Jesus' tomb were the only ones to be there for His resurrection (others would see Him after His resurrection). They came rushing to the religious leaders to bring the shocking news. Because the Jewish leaders were determined to squelch any talk that He arose, they came up with a scheme to say just that:

> Now after the Sabbath, as it began to dawn toward the first day of the week, Mary Magdalene and the other Mary came to look at the grave. And behold, a severe earthquake had occurred, for an angel of the Lord descended from heaven and came and rolled away the stone and sat upon it. And his appearance was like lightning, and his clothing as white as snow. The guards shook for fear of him and became like dead men. (Matthew 28:1–4)

> Now while they were on their way, some of the guard came into the city and reported to the chief priests all that had happened. And when they had assembled with the elders and consulted together, they gave a large sum of money to the soldiers, and said, "You are to say, 'His disciples came by night and stole Him away while we were asleep.' And if this should come to the governor's ears, we will win him over and keep you out of trouble." And they took the money and did as they had been instructed; and this story was widely spread among the Jews, and is to this day. (vv. 11–15)

Then as the disciples began to preach the crucified and risen Christ as the only way of salvation, the religious leaders really became furious. Peter preached, "Let it be known to all of you and to all the people of

Israel, that by the name of Jesus Christ the Nazarene, whom you crucified, whom God raised from the dead—by this name this man stands here before you in good health. He is the STONE WHICH WAS REJECTED by you, THE BUILDERS, but WHICH BECAME THE CHIEF CORNER stone. And there is salvation in no one else; for there is no other name under heaven that has been given among men by which we must be saved" (Acts 4:10–12).

The Jewish religious leaders began to imprison Christians to stop this teaching. But the apostles could not stop preaching the truth because they had seen Jesus alive. As they were threatened with death if they didn't stop preaching this (and many of them began to be martyred), death held no fear for them because they had seen Him alive. Death had been defeated.

Yet in spite of this, over the course of the first century, most Jews refused to believe that Jesus was their long-awaited Messiah. They did not believe He was God or rose from the dead even though the historical evidence was great that He did.

ANTI-SEMITISM

Sadly, due to these historical events some Christians have been seduced by the devil into anti-Semitism. Some have called the Jews "Christ kill-ers," while blind to the reality that Jesus was Jewish. All His disciples were Jewish. Most of His early followers were Jewish. Yes, Jewish religious lead-ers led many of the Jews to call for Jesus' crucifixion, but they simply represent all mankind who refuse to repent of sin and claim God's grace and mercy through faith in Jesus as the crucified and risen Lord. Anti-Semitism raised its ugly head in some of the early church fathers. It raised its ugly head during the Crusades. And saddest of all, many Christians did nothing to stop the devil-filled Adolf Hitler and his Nazi goons as they called Jews "Christ killers" as a justification for their satanic hatred of God's chosen people. All this has caused many a Jewish heart to become understandably harder in rejecting Jesus—*Yeshua*—as their Messiah.

If you are a Christian and in the slightest way are seduced by the devil into anti-Semitic thought, may you fall on your knees and confess this abominable sin to the Lord. Ask His forgiveness for such a sickening sin, and ask God to cleanse your heart of such evil. Remember, Jesus taught that He came first for the Jews (Matthew 15:24). And yes, He taught that He is "the way, and the truth, and the life; no one comes to the Father but through [Him]" (John 14:6). Every person—Jew or Gentile—has to answer to Christ's claims about Himself.

The Christian's calling is to love and pray for all who don't believe in Him and leave judgment up to God. We should learn from that great Jew, the apostle Paul, who wrote that he had great sorrow and unceasing grief in his heart for his Jewish brethren who refused to change their minds about Jesus and trust Him and follow Him as Savior and Lord (Romans 9:2–3). Paul went on to say that he was willing to be damned for the sake of his Jewish brethren if it meant they would change their minds and follow Christ. That is the spirit God wants us to have for the people He loves so much—a passionate love, and a passionate heart, for each Jewish person to know the love of Christ.

Yet as sad as it is that some Christians through the ages have fallen into the sin of anti-Semitism, it is in the heart and soul of Islam. And sadly, it is not seen as evil. We'll look at this as we examine the Islamic perspective.

10

THE ISLAMIC PERSPECTIVE

He [Ishmael] will be a wild donkey of a man, / His hand will be against everyone, / And everyone's hand will be against him; / And he will live to the east of all his brothers.

—GENESIS 16:12

Chronologically, Christianity flows out of Judaism. Islam came more than six hundred years later. But I chose to skip over the Christian perspective to the Islamic perspective, for the greatest conflict in the Middle East is between Jews and Muslims, between Israel and Arabs, between Muslims and Muslims. Christianity originated between these two influential faiths, and it has been caught in the middle between the two to this very day. The followers of Jesus Christ know how this conflict will finally be resolved, but first we must understand more of the Islamic perspective.

Of the three Abrahamic faiths, Islam was last to come onto the world scene. This religion did not appear until the seventh century AD—more than six hundred years after the life of Christ. Islam was founded by Muhammad and was originally seen by him not as a new religion but as a purification and completion of Judaism and Christianity that had been corrupted by man. Even though Islam and its holy book, the Qur'an, contain many references from the Old and New Testaments, these passages have been noticeably changed. Because much of his teaching was so contrary to Scripture, Muhammad faced resistance from Jews and Christians alike.

Originally Jerusalem was not an important place to Muhammad and Islam. Mecca and Medina, in modern-day Saudi Arabia, were and still are much more so. But when legends began to spread of Muhammad's ascension to heaven from what is now the site of the Dome of the Rock, Jerusalem became a much more important city. Now the Dome of the Rock is the third holiest site in all of Islam.

Like Judaism and Christianity, Islam sees Abraham as the father of the faith, the original prophet sent by God. But unlike Judaism and Christianity, Islam's focus of veneration among Muslims after Abraham is Ishmael, not Isaac. This is understandable, for Ishmael was the elder son of Abraham. He is also the father of the Arabs and thus, eventually, of Muhammad. The Qur'an was written in Arabic. Any translation into other languages is looked upon warily by Muslims, for only in Arabic can its pure meaning be understood.[1]

THE ARABS BEGIN WITH ISHMAEL

Remember, from Ishmael came the Arabs. From Esau came the Edomites and much of Jordan. From the Assyrians and Babylonians came much of what is Syria and Iraq today. From the Persians came Iran.

Yet from Ishmael is where we begin. When Hagar, Ishmael's Egyptian mother, first fled from her mistress, Sarah, God said that the child she was carrying would be named Ishmael (meaning "God hears"). God heard Hagar's troubles and had mercy on her. But that is not all God said. As we have already seen, God prophesied that her son, Ishmael, would be:

> *A wild donkey of a man.*
> *His hand will be against everyone,*
> *And everyone's hand will be against him;*
> *And he will live to the east of all his brothers.* (Genesis 16:12)

Later Genesis 25:18 clarifies where "east of all his brothers" was: "They settled from Havilah to Shur which is east of Egypt as one goes toward Assyria." In short, Arabia.

But the heart of this prophecy is that Ishmael and his heirs would be a restless people—untamable and constantly at odds with others. The first two millennia saw the heirs of Ishmael as largely nomadic Bedouin tribes that intermarried and fought with the Edomites, Amorites, Moabites, and others who inhabited the promised land and Arabia.

THE BEGINNING OF ISLAM

About twenty-five hundred years after Ishmael, in AD 570, a young Arab heir was born. This man would move the prophecy of Ishmael in Genesis 16:12 to a new level. His name was Muhammad.

Muhammad was an orphan. His father died before he was born. His mother died when he was six. His grandfather took him in for two years after that, and then he died. So little Muhammad went to live with an uncle who raised him.[2]

As a young man, he "gained the patronage of a wealthy widow," and eventually they were married, though she was fifteen years older than Muhammad.[3] Their marriage lasted twenty-five years before she died. It was evidently a very devoted and monogamous marriage. Ergun and Emir Caner, in their enlightening book *Unveiling Islam*, wrote, "Only later [after his wife's death] did Muhammad have eleven other women as wives and concubines, the youngest of whom was nine when they consummated their marriage."[4]

During the fifteenth year of his first marriage, when Muhammad was forty years old, he received his first revelation while meditating in a favorite cave. He had been deeply troubled at the spiritual and moral culture of his hometown in Mecca. The people there were prosperous yet polytheistic and full of pagan traditions. Their culture was overrun with one tribe fighting another. It was a constant picture of bloody violence and revenge. Islamic scholar Karen Armstrong has written, "Arabia was a chronically violent society."[5] It was the embodiment of God's prophecy of Ishmael in Genesis 16:12.

In the first revelation, Muhammad said that the angel Gabriel spoke to him. It is interesting to note that Gabriel was the angel who appeared to Mary, mother of Jesus, to announce her supernatural conception of the Son of God when she was a virgin. A comparison reveals that much of what is found in Islam and the Qur'an has been taken from Old and New Testament stories, though close study will show that many details have been changed.

At first, these revelations were frightening to Muhammad. His whole body would go into convulsions. He would sweat profusely and hear strange sounds and voices. He wasn't sure at first if they were from Allah (the Arabic name for God) or the devil. He even wondered if he had been possessed by an evil spirit. Yet when he shared his revelations with his devoted wife, she was impressed and believed it could be from God. She took him to see a cousin of hers who believed in one God and was well versed in the Jewish and Christian Holy Scriptures.[6] He felt the revelation was legitimate.

Yet even with this encouragement, at first Muhammad was cautious. He didn't seem to believe he was starting a new religion, just receiving revelations to bring purification to old ones. In the Qur'an, he is quoted as saying, "I am not an innovation among the messengers, nor do I know what will be done with me or with you. I follow but that which is revealed to me by inspiration" (Sura 46:9).[7] But after two to three years (the time frame is disputed), Muhammad began to share his revelations with others, and he was joined by the first converts to what would become a new religion. It would be called Islam, which means "submission"—total submission to Allah.

Yet as is often the case, people groups were reluctant to let go of their culture and religious beliefs. It was no different in Mecca. The people there did not want to give up their many gods for one god, Allah. Many thought Muhammad was crazy and a bad influence on their culture. It got so bad that he was run out of town, and he and his small group of fol-lowers escaped to Medina in AD 622.[8] Medina held a special place within Islam and is now Islam's second holiest site, after Mecca. In Medina, Muhammad moved from an itinerate prophet with new monotheistic religious ideas to the founder of a combination of a new religion and a militant state.[9] What caused this?

THE HOSTILITY OF THE JEWS

When he arrived in Medina, Muhammad was drawn to the large Jewish community and their monotheistic belief in one true God. He began to teach his band of Muslims to copy some of the religious practices of the Jews—like praying toward Jerusalem several times a day and not eating pork.

But over time, the Jews rejected his teaching when they saw how dif-ferent it was from biblical teaching. This embittered Muhammad, and his teaching began to take on a strong hostility to the Jews. He is quoted in the Qur'an as saying, "Strongest among men in enmity to Believers [Muslims] will you find the Jews and Pagans" (Sura 5:82). He also said, "Those who dis-believe, among the People of the Book [Jews] and among the Polytheistics, will be in hell-fire, to dwell therein. They are the worst of creatures" (Sura 98:6). Since the Qur'an is a compilation of the teachings of Muhammad, his teaching concerning the Jews is adhered to by his genuine followers today. This has caused Islam to be drenched with hatred of the Jews because the Qur'an is the absolute infallible Holy Book of Islam.[10]

From this time in Medina, Muhammad began to see the Jews as "devious and treacherous people, who had persecuted past prophets and falsified the Holy Scriptures."[11] This change is a classic example of a half-truth. Yes, the Bible is clear: Jewish people persecuted and rejected some of the prophets God sent to them (Jeremiah most comes to mind), but they *never* falsified Holy Scriptures of the Old Testament. This is a classic example of a devil-inspired half-truth to justify hatred of the Jews.

Muhammad saw that Christians and Jews had clarity about their deity, and the Arabs did not. So he took biblical teaching and adjusted it to build his own religion.

Jews had their Sabbath on Saturday. Christians worshipped on Sunday. So Muhammad made Friday the Muslim Sabbath. This makes traveling to Jerusalem today very interesting, since three different Sabbaths are visibly observed among the population. Jews used the trumpet to call people to prayer three times a day toward Jerusalem, so Muslims would pray more (five times a day), and they would be called to prayer by muezzins and minarets—a haunting sound that can be heard from mosques all over the world today. And no longer would Muslims pray toward Jerusalem, but toward Mecca, Muhammad's Arabic hometown. But it was not just his teaching that copied and tried to outdo the Jews. It was his actions that showed the greatest hostility.

In the spring of AD 627, Muhammad led his band of Muslims to murder between six hundred and eight hundred Jewish men of Medina. The Jews were brought in small groups and ordered to sit on the edge of the trenches dug the previous day, where they were beheaded and their bodies pushed into the trenches.[12] Like a scene out of the Holocaust of Nazi Germany during World War II depicting intense hatred toward the Jews, this is a mind-set derived straight from the pits of hell.

ISLAMIC UTOPIANISM

Later Muhammad returned to Mecca and was victorious. He became the city's dominant influence and Arabia's most powerful leader.[13] Emboldened by his success, believing it to be a sign of Allah's blessing, he no longer saw himself as just one messenger in a long line of messengers of God but the final and ultimate prophet of God. He became much more demonizing of those who opposed him. In his farewell address shortly before he died, Muhammad said, "I was ordered to fight all men until they say, 'There is no god but Allah.'" Remember, Islam (which means "total submission to Allah") was founded in blood and violence. Originally Muhammad wanted to unify and purify Arab religion under submission to the one and only God, Allah. But by the time of his death, he had taken on a classic utopian outloook. Whatever blood and violence is shed against the infidels who oppose them is justified to fulfill this utopian dream.

In light of this history the Western world was foolish to conclude that a man like Ayatollah Khomeini of Iran was just a Muslim extremist when he said of Iran's revolution in 1979, "We will export our revolution throughout the world . . . until the calls, 'There is no god but Allah and Muhammad is the messenger of Allah' are echoed all over the world."[14] Or that Osama bin Laden was just an Islamic extremist when he said about the 9/11 terrorist attack, "I was ordered to fight the people until they say there is no god but Allah."[15] These Muslim men are just following the teaching and vision of their founder.

What the world is facing from Islam in the twenty-first century is what the world faced in the twentieth century from the utopian approach of Marxism and Nazism. When I've shared this statement with people, it is often met with incredulous bewilderment. "How can this be, especially because Marxism is atheistic and Islam claims to be the true religion of Allah?" But they are all utopian dreams that believe that there will be no peace in this world until everyone submits to their ideology. In Islam, as it was in Marxism and Nazism, the end justifies the means if it advances their ideology and utopian dream. That includes murder. Nazism was steeped in hatred of the Jews, as is Islam. Both Nazism and Marxism, like Islam, are about winning people to their viewpoint, not through love and persuasion, but by power, force, intimidation, and fear. Speaking out about the evils of Islam in an Islamic society brings the same result it brought in Soviet Russia in speaking about the evils of Joseph Stalin, or in China on the murderous evil of Mao, or in Nazi Germany in speaking of the demonic evil of Adolf Hitler. Yes, the twentieth century had an atheistic utopian ideology that is proving to be very short-lived, as it dies a pitiful death on the ash heap of history. But in the twenty-first century, the utopian ideology is enveloped in an even worse evil, for it incorporates the holy name of God. Thus, all who oppose it and speak the truth of its evil are seen as opposing God himself.

THE SPREAD OF ISLAM

Yet what so many Westerners are so blind to is this utopian ideology of the twenty-first century is not a new development. It goes back fourteen hundred years. The utopianism of Islam advanced rapidly in the seventh century like a raging fire across Arabia. This advance was through military conquests.

But it did not stop there. The great scholar of Islam, Bernard Lewis of Princeton University, has written how Islam went beyond Arabia to conquer Syria, Palestine, Egypt, and North Africa, also in the seventh century. What many Christians do not realize is that these were all Christian strongholds before this occurred.[16]

When the Muslims conquered Jerusalem, it was important to them because of Abraham. Muhammad called Abraham the original prophet of Islam, which is why he is seen as the father of the three most influential religions of the world. But later in that century, in AD 691, when Muslims completed the Dome of the Rock on the site where Abraham had been willing to sacrifice his son to God, they believed it showed the superiority of Allah over the God of the Jews.

What is also enlightening is that even though the Qur'an never specifically says this, Islamic tradition holds that Ishmael, not Isaac, was the son that Abraham was willing to sacrifice to Allah. On that special rock on which the sacrifice was to occur sits the Dome of the Rock.

Obviously, this is just another example of the false teaching and counterfeit nature of Islam. Islam is even known to speak of Noah, Abraham, and Ishmael as followers of Allah. This is bizarre, since Islam didn't even exist when they lived. Islam and the Arab culture see Ishmael, as the elder son of Abraham, as the rightful heir. Of course, all of this serves to make the Dome of the Rock a holier site to Islam.

Lewis went on to note that in the eighth century, Muslims conquered Spain and Portugal. It was truly a religion on the move. In their minds, these continued conquests reinforced the superiority of Allah.

They continued on and invaded France, and, as I shared in chapter 1, if France had not turned back the Muslim onslaught in AD 732, most of Europe and eventually North and South America could have easily been dominated by the Muslim faith.

Another truth that many Westerners do not realize is this: not only does military success testify to the superiority of Allah to Muslims, but losses are simply seen as merely temporary setbacks to fulfilling their dream of bringing the entire world under submission to Allah. In the Arabic and Muslim world, the focus is on power, especially military power. So when losses come, it doesn't mean Muslims will quit or accept defeat. Instead, they are waiting until they have the right amount of power and possible change in strategy to advance forward. For instance, Islam is rapidly growing in Europe today, not through military might, but through immigration and high birth rates.[17] It is growing so rapidly that, within this century, Muslims could easily become the majority people group in many European nations. Muammar Qadhafi commented on this change in strategy: "There are signs that Allah will grant Islam victory in Europe—without swords, without guns, without conquests."[18]

This patient waiting for the right amount of power to advance Islam was seen in the ninth century when Arab Muslims came at Europe from a different direction. They attacked and conquered Sicily, and by 846 they had sacked Rome.[19] What historians rarely note is the fear that was created within the center of Western Christianity that set the stage for the very misguided vision of the Crusades. It was during this time the church adopted a very Islamic mind-set of unifying the state and the church in Holy War.[20]

The Crusades were staged from 1095 to 1291 to "rescue" the Holy Land. Yet when Islam finally triumphed, it was once again vindication for Allah. Muslims saw their land under siege, and they believed Allah gave them the victory. If there is one thing that emboldens Muslim Arabs, it is victory. They consider victory a sign that the "infidels" (non-Muslims) have grown weak.

At this point in history no force in the world seemed stronger than Islam. Bernard Lewis wrote that it was the greatest military power on earth. And along with military might they were the world's greatest merchants and had achieved high levels in the arts and sciences.[21]

Even when Genghis Khan's Mongol hordes advanced westward in central Asia, in what is today Iraq, and conquered those lands, they converted to Islam and were eventually defeated.[22] And then in the fourteenth century, the Ottoman Empire (the Turks) began to dominate Islam. By 1453, the Ottomans conquered Constantinople (now Istanbul), which was the eastern headquarters of Christianity and the final stronghold of the Eastern Roman Empire known as Byzantium. It was one of the saddest days in Christian history. When the cross on top of what had been the largest Christian cathedral in the world, the Hagia Sophia, was taken down, it symbolized to Muslims the greatness of Allah and Islam over all of Christianity. At this point, it seemed nothing could stop the mighty power and spread of Islam. None of this should be a surprise in light of God's promise to Abraham in Genesis 17:20: "As for Ishmael, I have heard you; behold, I will bless him, and will make him fruitful and will multiply him exceedingly. He shall become the father of twelve princes, and I will make him a great nation." God promised Abraham that He would build a great nation or people group from Ishmael. What He did not explain to Abraham was all the long-term turmoil that would result from God's being merciful to Abraham despite his not waiting on God for a son.

EUROPE RISES IN IMPORTANCE

Then came 1492 and a huge momentum shift. Americans know 1492 as the year that Ferdinand and Isabella of Spain commissioned an Italian explorer named Christopher Columbus to sail west toward what he thought was India. As we now know, he discovered a different type of

Indian. But it was also the year that marked what Christianity felt was a purification of Spain. After eight centuries of Islamic rule, the Muslims were expelled. And sadly, as was often the case for well-meaning Christians in the so-called Holy Wars, Jews were victimized in the process. They were terribly mistreated in the Crusades; Christian invaders would kill Jews and burn synagogues as they came to fight the Muslims and claim the land for the church. And later in 1492, every Jew was expelled from Spain. It was a very black day in the history of Christendom.

With the momentum shift of 1492, so-called Christian Europe moved to the forefront of development and civilization. Even though Suleiman the Magnificent would lead the Ottoman Empire to its greatest days in the sixteenth century, Muslims were put on the defensive when the Ottoman Turks failed to take Vienna in 1529. The victory in Spain seemed to motivate Europe into an age of colonial expansion into Africa and North and South America. Europe moved into the golden age of the Renaissance, and Islam began to retreat to Central Asia and the Middle East and North Africa, which it saw as a time of inner strengthening under the unity the Turks brought to much of Islam. This continued until the early part of the twentieth century, until World War I.[23]

Paul Johnson wrote, "Throughout the nineteenth century it had usually been British policy to treat Turkey, 'the sick man of Europe,' gently and try to keep its crumbling empire together. All that changed when Turkey [Muslim Ottomans] joined Germany in 1914."[24] After World War I, Saudi Arabia quickly rushed in to claim the Arabian Peninsula when Turkey collapsed, slaughtering all in their path—the prophecy of Ishmael being fulfilled again. "Then it became Anglo-French policy to strip Turkey of its Arab provinces and divide the spoils."[25] Out of this, France got Syria and Lebanon, and Britain got Palestine and Transjordan. The young war minister from Britain who led much of this process of dividing up the Middle East spoils was named Winston Churchill. While in Egypt (which was then under British rule), he literally drew up new kingdoms on the map.

Suddenly, new nations—called Transjordan (Jordan) and Iraq—appeared. With Britain controlling India and much of the Middle East,

Churchill would often boast, "The British Empire is the world's greatest Muslim power."[26]

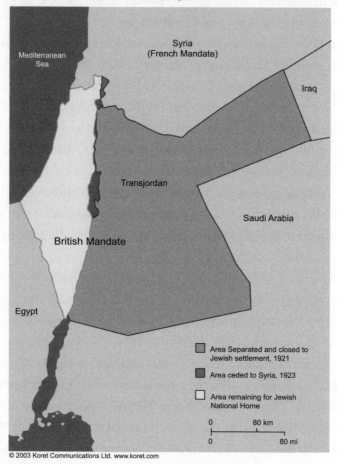

1922: Separation of Transjordan

Syria (French Mandate)

Mediterranean Sea

Iraq

Transjordan

Saudi Arabia

British Mandate

Egypt

☐ Area Separated and closed to Jewish settlement, 1921

■ Area ceded to Syria, 1923

☐ Area remaining for Jewish National Home

0   80 km

0   80 mi

© 2003 Koret Communications Ltd. www.koret.com

All this humiliated Muslims in the Middle East, and worst of all, it was a humiliation to Allah. But the Brits were not finished. In 1917, Britain issued the Balfour Declaration, described in chapter 1, calling for a national homeland for the Jews in Palestine. Churchill, as the foreign minister of Britain, was an enthusiastic supporter.[27] The Arab Muslim world was appalled. When they conquered Jerusalem in AD 638 in the early days of Islam, they had staked their claim for Allah on Jerusalem. This was illustrated emphatically with the building of the Dome of the Rock on the site of the ancient temple of the Jews just over forty years later, in 691. In their minds, this proved Allah's superiority over the Jewish God. Yet with the Balfour Declaration, Britain and its biblical Christian heritage led the way for the vision that was already embraced by many leading Jewish Zionists in Europe.

Then after World War II and the world's horror in the realization of the Holocaust and the accompanying guilt that went with it, the United Nations gave approval for a national homeland for the Jews in Palestine. On May 14, 1948, Israel was reborn. The Arab Muslim world was outraged, and as we've seen, five Arab Muslim nations around Israel immediately declared war on Israel to drive the Jews into the sea.

Yet here we are in the twenty-first century, and Israel has survived despite being overwhelmingly outnumbered and surrounded by Arab Muslim nations that despise her very existence. Because of this, the humiliation to Arab Muslims and Allah himself has only intensified.

All this might seem like a crash course in world history, but to the biblical Jew and Christian, it is a reminder that God is orchestrating the events of history. It seems that man's political games and military victories determine the decisions, but God is in charge.

SUPREMACY WITHIN ISLAM

But there is more to the story. When President Ahmadinejad of Iran calls for Israel to be wiped off the face of the earth, it is not just hatred of the Jews that motivates him. It is also not just to fulfill his Islamic Shiite apocalyptic utopian vision. It is a cry to rally the Muslim world under the leadership of Iran. For since the fall of the Ottoman Empire at the end of World War I, there has been a vacuum of leadership in the Muslim world.

The Saudis initially wanted to make that claim, especially in Arabia when the Turks fell. Yet the Brits were able to keep them in check to just a portion of Arabia.

Then in the 1950s, Abdul Nasser rose to power in Egypt. He had a "Pan-Arabic nationalist dream. He aimed to become the preeminent leader of a united Islamic world, and Israel was the perfect foil for his ambitions . . . In July of 1956, Egypt nationalized the Suez Canal and blockaded the Strait of Tiran. Israel's access to Africa and Asia was crippled. [Then] the Egyptian army began taking up portions in the Negev (south of Israel)."[28] That same month, Egypt signed an agreement with Syria and Jordan that made Nasser the leader of their forces. He then issued this statement: "Egypt has decided to dispatch her heroes, the disciples of Pharaoh and the sons of Islam and they will cleanse the land of Palestine. We demand vengeance and vengeance is Israel's death . . . Our hatred is very strong. There is no sense talking about peace with Israel."[29]

With Israel so threatened, she launched a preemptive attack on Egypt under prime minister David Ben-Gurion on October 29, 1956. About a week later, Israel had captured the entire Sinai region and ended the blockade of the Strait of Tiran. A miracle? Yes. Yet once again for the Arab Muslim world—humiliation.

Then came the Six-Day War in 1967. Once again Muslim Arab forces were poised to strike. Egypt was gathering its forces along Israel's southern border, and Syrian troops were poised to strike along the Golan Heights overlooking northern Israel around Galilee. Nasser, still president of Egypt, wrote as a good Muslim Arab about how this time they were poised to win because they had the power. He said, "We were waiting for the day when we would be fully prepared and confident. Recently we felt we are strong enough, that if we were to enter a battle with Israel, with God's help, we could triumph."[30]

Once again, Israel's very existence was threatened. And once again her preemptive strike destroyed Egypt and Syrian air forces before they even got off the ground. The world remembers this as the Six-Day War, another miraculous Israeli triumph. In this war, Israel captured the Sinai and Golan Heights and much of the West Bank and all of Jerusalem. This total liberation of Jerusalem allowed Israel to claim the temple mount. Tears of joy overflowed among the Jews in Israel to now control what they had lost in AD 70 to Rome.

Then came the Yom Kippur War in 1973, which caught Israel off guard. The Arabs launched an attack on Yom Kippur, the Jews' holiest day of the year, when the nation is mostly shut down and worshipping and in prayer at the synagogue or spending time with family. Yet Israel miraculously fought back and was spared once again. The miracles of survival and triumph over hostile forces just keep on coming.

It was one thing for Europe to hold the spread of Islam at bay. But for little-bitty Israel from May 14, 1948, with a Jewish population of about 650,000, to hold off hundreds of millions of Arab Muslims all around them and do it again and again in the '50s and '60s and '70s was total humiliation to the Muslim world.

In light of God's promise to Abraham almost four thousand years earlier, "I will bless those who bless you, and the one who curses you I will curse" (Genesis 12:3), biblical Christians and Jews have been amazed but not surprised. For one who believes the promises of God's Word, the foolishness of being on the wrong side of history against God's chosen people is very clear indeed.

But the vacuum of leadership in the Muslim world continued. In the 1980s, Saddam Hussein and Iraq fought a bloody war with Ayatollah Khomeini and Iran. The war was fought to a standstill, but the real issue was supremacy in the Muslim world.

Then in the early 1990s, Saddam switched strategies and invaded Kuwait. With his war with the United States (the major supporter of Israel) and her allies, Saddam tried to rally the Arab Muslims around him. It failed. He was soundly defeated.

Now, is there any doubt what Ahmadinejad and Iran are up to? Leadership of the Muslim world is the goal, and hatred of Israel and the Jews fuels the fire. Yet Muslims in Egypt and Saudi Arabia are opposed to Iran. Why is that the case? For one thing, this is about Islamic supremacy between Arabs and Persians, but there is even more.

SUNNIS VERSUS SHIITES

After Muhammad died in AD 632, a huge power struggle ensued for the leadership of Islam. Some thought Muslim leadership ought to be limited to direct descendants of Muhammad. These Muslims became known as Shiites. Other Muslims felt the leadership should be in the hands of caliphs—spiritual leaders who may or may not have any direct kinship with Muhammad. These Muslims are called Sunnis, and they make up almost 90 percent of the Muslim world.[31] Shiites dominate in Iran and Iraq, although Saddam Hussein and his Sunni factor strong-armed them into submission under his rule.

Day after day Americans and the Western world are bewildered to see Muslim terrorist suicide bombers bombing Muslims. Sometimes this happens even while Muslims are worshipping in their mosques. Yet really it is the ultimate example of the fulfillment of God's prophecy of Ishmael and his heirs in Genesis 16:12:

> He will be a wild donkey of a man,
> His hand will be against everyone,
> And everyone's hand will be against him.

Arabs against Jews. Arabs against Arabs. Arabs against Persians. Muslims against Jews. Muslims against Christians. Muslims against Muslims.

Do we throw up our hands in disgust and hopelessness at this seemingly irresolvable violence? Absolutely not! Christians believe there is ultimate hope in one person—Jesus Christ. He not only is the Prince of Peace, but He has come to be the Savior of Jews and Arabs and Muslims and all of mankind.

This leads us to our next chapter on the Christian perspective as we consider the Middle East conflict. In the Christian perspective we see the man in the middle often caught in the crossfire.

11

THE CHRISTIAN PERSPECTIVE

She will bear a Son; and you shall call His name Jesus,
for He will save His people from their sins.

—MATTHEW 1:21

The Christian perspective begins with the birth of Jesus Christ. The New Testament contains Christian beliefs that flow out of the Old Testament and the Jewish faith. The New Testament is essentially divided into four parts:

- THE GOSPELS tell of the birth, life, death, burial, and resurrection of Jesus Christ, the long-awaited Messiah of Israel who is also God's Son, the Savior and Lord.
- ACTS OF THE APOSTLES tells of the birth of the church and its early history, focused mostly on the apostles Peter and Paul.
- THE EPISTLES (letters to the early churches) teach doctrine (how to believe in Jesus) and how to live for Him. The apostle Paul wrote most of these, though the apostles Peter and John, along with others, contributed some letters as well.
- THE REVELATION that Christ gave to the apostle John teaches of the events leading up to Jesus' Second Coming and the end

times. It is rich in symbolism and is perhaps the most difficult book to understand.

The early church was overwhelmingly Jewish. Jesus and all the disciples were Jewish. Traditional Jews and Jews who followed Jesus as Messiah and God's Son split apart in the first century. The apostle Paul was a leading traditional Jew from a Jewish aristocratic background before his conversion to follow Christ. Very soon, the church became overwhelmingly Gentile with just a remnant of Jewish followers of Jesus, and this continues to be the case to this very day.

Over time, Rome and Constantinople (now Istanbul) became the two most important centers for the church. Yet for biblical Christians, no city compares with Jerusalem in importance, for Christ was crucified and rose from the dead there. This represents the heart and soul of the Christian faith.

THE LITTLE TOWN OF BETHLEHEM

The little town of Bethlehem holds a unique place in Jewish and Christian heritage. Yet Bethlehem is currently under the control of the Palestinian Authority and Islam.

Bethlehem is the site where the Jewish patriarch Jacob's beloved wife, Rachel, died. It is the site of the romantic story of Ruth and Boaz, described so beautifully in the book of Ruth. It is the birthplace of a Jewish boy who tended sheep on the hills and grew up to be King David, the greatest of all of Israel's kings. And the Jewish prophet Micah prophesied that the Messiah of the Jews, who would inherit the throne of King David, would be born in this little town of Bethlehem:

> "But as for you, Bethlehem Ephrathah,
> Too little to be among the clans of Judah,
> From you One will go forth for Me to be ruler in Israel.
> His goings forth are from long ago,
> From the days of eternity." (Micah 5:2)

The Gospels of Matthew and Luke describe how Jesus was born in Bethlehem as a fulfillment of Micah's prophecy. Matthew says that when the wise men from the East (probably Persia) saw the star and came to Jerusalem, searching for where the King of the Jews had been born, the Jewish scribes and chief priests were clear: the Messiah would be born in Bethlehem.

Today, Bethlehem is a very sad place. With the Palestinian Muslim control of the town, Christian Arabs are quickly being squeezed out. The *Wall Street Journal* on December 28, 2009, ran the article "The Forgotten Palestinian Refugees." They chronicled how Palestinian Christians are being squeezed out by the Muslims with the backing of the Palestinian Authority. In the mid-twentieth century, Christian Palestinians made up about 80 percent of Bethlehem's population. That percentage has now shrunk to about 20 percent, largely because of Christian emigration.[1]

I'll never forget the fear and anxiety on the face of one of our Christian Arab tour guides after the Muslims had taken control of the town. We asked him to explain the situation as we stood outside the church in Bethlehem that commemorates the site of Jesus' birth. He began to sweat profusely and said he couldn't talk about it. Later on the tour in the sanctuary of the beautiful Church of the Nativity, we asked him once again, "Could you level with us on the situation?" The poor, kind man began to sweat again, and then tears welled up in his eyes. "It is not good," he said. "We don't know how much longer we can stay. My family is making plans to escape. It breaks our hearts, for this is our home, the birthplace of our Lord. But I really shouldn't say any more. If they hear me, my whole family could be in danger." We asked him, "Can we pray for you now?" He said, "Please." Many in our group that day were weeping for the man and for the situation, for it is hard to describe the tension we felt that day in Bethlehem.

I share this with you, for I believe Bethlehem is a metaphor for the tension and conflict in the Middle East today. I'll never forget what a thriving little town Bethlehem was when it was under Israeli control. Today it is an oppressive environment with boarded-up shops and hostile stares.

I believe Bethlehem thrived under Israeli control because of the shared Jewish and Christian biblical heritage. And I believe it is a place of great sadness and tension today for the very nature of Islam, its name, its founder, its belief is about bringing everyone into submission to Allah by force or intimidation.

THE TENSION IN BETHLEHEM

From the time Jesus entered the world in the little town of Bethlehem, there has been a great tension. It is understandable that Christians love to focus on the good news and joy of His birth. We love to reflect on how He was worshipped in those early days after His birth, and we should. The celebration and joy of a Savior's birth in the City of David was great. The shepherds came and were filled with joy. The wise men from the East worshipped Him as Lord. But Christians often overlook the "rest of the story." What followed was great tension in Bethlehem after Jesus entered the world and the wise men headed home.

And having been warned by God in a dream not to return to Herod, the magi left for their own country by another way.

Now when they had gone, behold, an angel of the Lord appeared to Joseph in a dream and said, "Get up! Take the Child and His mother, and flee to Egypt, and remain there until I tell you; for Herod is going to search for the Child to destroy Him."

So Joseph got up and took the Child and His mother while it was still night, and left for Egypt. He remained there until the death of Herod. This was to fulfill what had been spoken by the Lord through the prophet: "OUT OF EGYPT I CALLED MY SON."

Then when Herod saw that he had been tricked by the magi, he became very enraged, and sent and slew all the male children who were in Bethlehem and all its vicinity, from two years old and under, according to the time which he had determined from the magi.

Then what had been spoken through Jeremiah the prophet was

fulfilled:

> "A VOICE WAS HEARD IN RAMAH,
>
> WEEPING AND GREAT MOURNING,
>
> RACHEL WEEPING FOR HER CHILDREN;
>
> AND SHE REFUSED TO BE COMFORTED,
>
> BECAUSE THEY WERE NO MORE."

But when Herod died, behold, an angel of the Lord appeared in a dream to Joseph in Egypt, and said,

"Get up, take the Child and His mother, and go into the land of Israel; for those who sought the Child's life are dead."

So Joseph got up, took the Child and His mother, and came into the land of Israel. (Matthew 2:12–21)

Many things are significant in this historical account. First, *God was obviously in control.* He is all-powerful. Herod wanted to kill Jesus, yet God intervened miraculously with the wise men first, then with Joseph, the earthly father and protector of Jesus.

Second, *God led them to Egypt.* The flight of Mary and Joseph and Jesus to Egypt would take them to the very place where their ancestors had been enslaved by Pharaoh after the days of Joseph (the eleventh son of Jacob [Israel]) until the days of Moses, their earthly redeemer. Now rather than being a place of enslavement, Egypt would be a sanctuary for our Lord. Quite a change for Egypt in the eyes of God after all the harsh judgment He had brought upon them for their enslavement of His specially chosen children, the Israelites. It is also fascinating because it was the fulfillment of biblical prophecy through the Jewish prophet Hosea, through whom God said, "When Israel was a youth I loved him, / And out of Egypt I called My son" (Hosea 11:1). Matthew just quotes the second part of the verse, but the first phrase reveals the unique relationship of Israel and God's Son. They are eternally entwined.

Third, *Herod wanted to eliminate Jesus.* A paranoid example of evil and cruelty, Herod wanted to eliminate anyone who was a threat to his power. But to see this from the standpoint of one man's evil and cruelty is to miss a much bigger part of this story. We'll see how that is, for there is so much more.

Fourth, *what Herod did in murdering the baby boys of Bethlehem was a despicable evil.* Yet this slaughter was prophesied by Jeremiah hundreds of years before Jesus' birth:

> *Thus says the* LORD,
> *"A voice is heard in Ramah,*
> *Lamentation and bitter weeping.*
> *Rachel is weeping for her children;*
> *She refuses to be comforted for her children,*
> *Because they are no more."* (Jeremiah 31:15)

Finally, *when Herod died, God led Joseph and Mary and young Jesus back to the promised land,* where His life story unfolds. Yet what is so rich about this background of the tension around Bethlehem after Jesus' birth is the unique relationship of Israel and Jesus with misguided worldly power and religions.

THE SIGN OF REVELATION 12

More prophetic words enlighten us to the tension of Bethlehem and Israel and Jesus and the Middle East and the world we live in. They are found in Revelation 12:1–6:

> A great sign appeared in heaven: a woman clothed with the sun, and the moon under her feet, and on her head a crown of twelve stars; and she was with child; and she cried out, being in labor and in pain to give birth. Then another sign appeared in heaven: and behold, a great red dragon having seven heads and ten horns, and on his heads were seven diadems. And his tail swept away a third of the stars of heaven and

threw them to the earth. And the dragon stood before the woman who was about to give birth, so that when she gave birth he might devour her child. And she gave birth to a son, a male child, who is to rule all the nations with a rod of iron; and her child was caught up to God and to His throne. Then the woman fled into the wilderness where she had a place prepared by God, so that there she would be nourished for one thousand two hundred and sixty days.

Revelation is overflowing with rich symbolism. Bible-believing Christians differ over the interpretation of many of the passages, but there are certain truths that should not be missed.

The Great Sign in Heaven

What is this "great sign" in heaven in verse 1? People interested in studies of end times often feel it refers to the signs in the heavens that mark the return of Christ as He shares His insight about this in Matthew 24:29–30: "But immediately after the tribulation of those days THE SUN WILL BE DARKENED, AND THE MOON WILL NOT GIVE ITS LIGHT, AND THE STARS WILL FALL from the sky, and the powers of the heavens will be shaken. And then the sign of the Son of Man will appear in the sky, and then all the tribes of the earth will mourn, and they will see the SON OF MAN COMING ON THE CLOUDS OF THE SKY with power and great glory." It certainly may be. But remember, biblical prophecy can speak to more than one event. We've seen this in the prophecy of Jeremiah and Ezekiel that speaks of the Jews one day returning to the land. The prophets were speaking to their contemporary age in prophesying how the Jews would be able to return to the promised land after the Babylonian captivity beginning in 538 BC. Little did they probably realize that as they spoke the timeless Word of God, they were speaking of the ingathering of the Jews to Israel that began en masse in the twentieth century. This really increased in 1948, but continues to this day.

In that light, I believe Revelation 12:1 is even more speaking of that star that was shown over Bethlehem. This was God's sign of Jesus' birth to the wise men.

Who Is this Woman?

There are three major interpretations of the woman described in Revelation 12:1–6. Some commentators say this woman is the church. But this is an erroneous understanding because Jesus gave birth to the church, not vice versa. Some say the woman is Mary, the mother of Jesus. Certainly it is Mary, but it is much, much more. Remember, prophecy so often contains layers of meaning. Mary was the chosen one of Israel to give birth to God's Son.

In this light, I believe the woman being described here is the nation of Israel. Israel is the one through whom God has chosen to give birth to His Son.

Certainly this woman is both Mary and Israel, but in this case most of all Israel. Why? God's Word speaks of this woman being clothed in the sun, with the moon under her feet and a crown of twelve stars on her head. Jacob's son Joseph, the dreamer, had a dream that really ticked off his brothers (especially his ten older brothers). Genesis 37:9 describes it: "Now he had still another dream, and related it to his brothers, and said, 'Lo, I have had still another dream; and behold, the sun and the moon and eleven stars were bowing down to me.'" It was a prophecy of his father Israel (the sun) and the moon (I'll let you speculate on who the moon is) and eleven stars (clearly his eleven brothers), who would one day represent, along with Joseph (through his son), the twelve tribes of Israel. From the twelve tribes of Israel comes the nation of Israel. This prophecy of the woman being Israel makes the most sense with the woman giving birth to God's Son. Mary was simply the personal representative of Israel.

You may be wondering, what does all this have to do with the Christian perspective on the Middle East conflict? Keep reading.

The Dragon and His Angels

In Revelation 12:3–4, another sign appears in heaven. This one is not good. It is biblically indisputable that this dragon is the devil and the stars he swept out of heaven with him were the angels who followed him. How do we know? The Bible tells us so.

> And there was war in heaven, Michael [the archangel] and his angels waging war with the dragon. The dragon and his angels waged war, and they were not strong enough, and there was no longer a place found for them in heaven. And the great dragon was thrown down, *the serpent of old who is called the devil and Satan*, who deceives the whole world; he was thrown down to the earth, and his angels were thrown down with him (Revelation 12:7–9; emphasis added).

This is a description of the devil's rebellion against God in heaven. Why? Because he wanted to supplant God. He was joined by one-third of the angels of heaven in this revolt. These angels are now called demons. No one knows exactly when this occurred, but it clearly occurred sometime before the first man and woman were created by God in the garden of Eden.

Yet as we see this eternal cosmic picture of bigger events taking place, let us not overlook the immediate historical event this describes: Jesus' birth in Bethlehem. The devil-filled man who sought to devour (or destroy) this child of God and of Israel was King Herod.

What is so interesting is that Herod was put in power by Rome somewhere around 40 BC. Rome certainly represented the ultimate in worldly power in that day. Like many rulers who are the picture of evil from a biblical perspective, Herod was extremely successful from a worldly perspective. His rebuilding (more significantly, we should say a complete renovation) of the second temple that was built after the Jews returned from their Babylonian exile was spectacular. Yet from God's Word, Herod is the embodiment of evil for what he wanted to do to Jesus, as well as how incredibly cruel he was to his fellow man.

Herod is a classic picture in miniature of the Antichrist. He represents megalomaniac rulers who want to rule and unify their kingdoms around themselves. Whether it was Nebuchadnezzar of Babylon, or Alexander the

Great of Macedonia, or Antiochus Epiphanes IV of Syria who desecrated the temple between 175–164 BC; or the Caesars of Rome in the first century; their spirit was the spirit of the Antichrist. In more recent history, Napoleon of France and Hitler of Germany and Stalin of Russia and Mao of China and even more recently, Saddam Hussein of Iraq have all had the same way of thinking—the mind-set of the devil: to usurp God with themselves and to unify their kingdoms around their self-glorification.

Again, what does all this have to do with the Christian perspective on the Middle East conflict? Read on. You're almost there.

What is so interesting about devil-filled Herod when he tried to destroy Jesus is his background. He was not only appointed by Rome, the chief worldly power of that day, but he was half-Jewish and half-Edomite. What Herod tried to do with Jesus in eliminating Him from the scene was a foreshadowing of what most of the Jewish religious leaders and some of the Jews of Jesus' day sought to do with the power of Rome through Jesus' crucifixion. To this day, most of their Jewish heirs continue to reject Jesus as God's Son and the Jewish Messiah. But it doesn't stop here, and if you are allowing the devil to start whispering anti-Semitic thoughts into your brain at this point, you are simply letting incomplete thoughts rush you to a misguided conclusion. Don't overlook the rest of the story.

Herod's Edomite heritage represents that people group who overwhelmingly came to follow the teaching of Muhammad, the most influential false prophet in the history of man. Their heirs who have embraced Islam have become enslaved to a false teaching that has and will continue to be the greatest hostility to Jesus and His followers.

What Muslims are doing today in the city of Jesus' birth, Bethlehem, they desire to do all over Israel, the Middle East, and ultimately in all the world.

To those misguided people who mistakenly use the analogy of the dragon in Revelation to justify hostility to the Jews, realize the woman who gave birth to Jesus is Israel, God's specially chosen people. Though the majority of Jews since the time of Jesus' birth in Bethlehem have rejected Him, they are still God's specially chosen people. God has not given up on them. The apostle Paul wrote, "I say then, God has not rejected His people, has He? May it never be! For I too am an Israelite, a descendant of Abraham, of the tribe of Benjamin" (Romans 11:1).

THE PROPHETIC PICTURE

But for now, don't miss the biblical and prophetic picture. God's Son could not be destroyed in Bethlehem by the devil through Herod. He could not be destroyed through His death on the cross outside Jerusalem. And one day He is coming again—this time to rule all the nations of the earth (Revelation 12:5a). But in the meantime, He has been resurrected and ascended to heaven where He reigns from the throne of God over all (Revelation 12:5b). What a glorious picture indeed! Yet there is more. Yes, more.

Verse 4 is very clear: the devil, who seeks to destroy Jesus, has also sought to destroy the people God loves all throughout history. These are the people who gave birth to Jesus. What then does verse 6 mean? Those who interpret Revelation 6–22 as future events believe this is prophecy that the Jews of modern-day Israel will flee to the wilderness during the time of the Great Tribulation. During those days, the final Antichrist will unleash his hatred on them. With the layers of meaning in prophecy, that certainly could be. Yet, it can describe more.

It could be describing Mary and Joseph's flight to Egypt with baby Jesus. Not a flight on an airplane, but fleeing from the devil-filled Herod.

It also describes in a very symbolic sense what happened to the Jews and Israel in AD 70–135, when Rome conquered Jerusalem and the temple was leveled. Jesus prophesied this shortly before His crucifixion while sitting with His disciples on the Mount of Olives looking out at the temple where the Dome of the Rock now stands. "Jesus came out from the temple and was going away when His disciples came up to point out the temple buildings to Him. And He said to them, 'Do you not see all these things? Truly I say to you, not one stone here will be left upon another, which will not be torn down'" (Matthew 24:1–2). Jesus' prophecy was fulfilled, and the Jews were expelled from the promised land and scattered to the nations of the world outside their land.

What all this has to do with the Christian perspective in the Middle East is from the time God's Son entered the world in Bethlehem as a child of Israel, the devil has sought to destroy Him. And because of God's love for Israel, where He chose to give birth to His son, the devil has sought to destroy the Jews and Israel, as well. This always ties the Jewish and Christian perspectives. They will always be joined in a special relationship.

Demonic opposition will continue until Jesus comes again and reigns with great power over all the nations of the world. And until Jesus comes, the conflict and tension in the Middle East will continue. Israel will face continued hostility from the world. And the source of so much of her tension will be the political dynamics of godless nations turning against her in an increasingly godless world. Along with this, Islam will continue to hate her. It will keep pushing to be in control and unify the world around the false god of Allah, and Israel will increasingly be seen with contempt.

THE CHRISTIAN RESPONSE

So what is the Christian to do in the face of the crisis in the Middle East? It all seems so hopeless. The conflict is humanly impossible to resolve. But remember, God is ultimately in charge of history. He has great plans for the Middle East.

Pray for the Peace of Jerusalem

God's Word commands this in Psalm 122:6:

> Pray for the peace of Jerusalem:
> "May they prosper who love you."

But if you'll look at that psalm, it says so much more:

> I was glad when they said to me,

"Let us go to the house of the LORD."
Our feet are standing
Within your gates, O Jerusalem,
Jerusalem, that is built
As a city that is compact together. (Psalm 122:1–3)

I really believe a Christian going to Jerusalem and standing within the gates develops a great love for the Jews and Israel. It is encouragement to the Jews and Israel that are increasingly alone in this world. "May peace be within your walls" (Psalm 122:7); "For the sake of the house of the LORD our God, / I will seek your good" (Psalm 122:9). Christians are to pray for Israel. To seek good for her. To be grateful for the common heritage we share.

Love Christ, and Follow His Teaching

The Christian's role is to love Christ and follow His teaching. Jesus' Great Commandment is clear: "'YOU SHALL LOVE THE LORD YOUR GOD WITH ALL YOUR HEART, AND WITH ALL YOUR SOUL, AND WITH ALL YOUR MIND.' This is the great and foremost commandment. The second is like it, 'YOU SHALL LOVE YOUR NEIGHBOR AS YOURSELF'" (Matthew 22:37–39). Romans 12:18 says, "If possible, so far as it depends on you, be at peace with all men." We are to love the Jews and be supportive of Israel, for God's Word commands us to do so. But we are also to love the Arab Muslims. Christ came to be the Savior of the world—Jew and Arab, Israeli and Muslim. He came to die for the sins of all mankind. This means praying for the Jews of Israel and the Arab Muslims to come to repentant faith in Christ so their hearts can be transformed from hatred to love, from revenge to forgiveness. The life-transforming power of the gospel of Jesus is the only way to do that. Christians are to seek to be a good and loving witness for Christ to Jews and Arabs and all mankind.

Pray for Christ's Return

Praying for the peace of Jerusalem means that, most of all, we are praying for Jesus to return. For both Judaism and Islam are strong on "an eye for an eye" teaching. They are short on the teaching of forgiveness and loving their enemies. Yet, this is central to Jesus and true Christianity. Jesus said, "You have heard that it was said, 'YOU SHALL LOVE YOUR NEIGHBOR and hate your enemy.' But I say to you, love your enemies and pray for those who persecute you" (Matthew 5:43–44).

The tension and hostility in the Middle East will continue between Jews and Arabs, between Jews and Muslims, between Israel and Muslim nations, between Muslims and Muslims until Jesus comes again to reign from His throne in Jerusalem over all the earth. Then and only then will there be true peace with perfect justice in the Middle East and in all the world.

"City of Jerusalem," courtesy of Paul and Donna Hearn

Yet amid all of this, the more we love God, the more we love His special people. My love for the Jewish people grows every time I go to Jerusalem and stand in the Garden of Gethsemane looking up to the sealed Eastern Gate in the wall of Jerusalem.

I long for that day when Jesus comes again and touches down on the Mount of Olives (Zechariah 14:4). He will then come down the mountain toward Jerusalem. At the base of the Mount of Olives is the Garden of Gethsemane. He will probably go by there. Maybe He will stop and pause, remembering the long night of agony He spent there, when He prayed for strength to fulfill His Father's will. What an agonizing night Jesus had before He was crucified. I wonder if He'll reflect a moment and think, *It was all worth it—the price I paid to save the souls of billions—and now is the day all the world has needed for so, so long. I have come.* I then see Him moving up Mount Moriah into the opened Eastern Gate to enter Jerusalem and begin to reign in perfect peace and justice to a worshipful and thankful world. Oh, come, Lord Jesus!

The Christian perspective on the Middle East is filled with hope. It's a hope that comes from the trustworthiness of God's Word. It's a hope that reminds us God is in control and that one day the jewel of the Middle East, Jerusalem, will truly be the center of all the world where Christ will reign on earth as He now reigns in heaven.

SOME FINAL THOUGHTS

Three Burning Questions

When presented with the facts regarding the biblical roots of the Middle East conflict, I find there are usually two or three vital questions that burn deep within people's hearts. These seem to be the most commonly asked.

QUESTION #1: DOES GOD PLAY FAVORITES?

The questioning usually begins with, "Does God play favorites?" In light of all the biblical teaching we have looked at, the answer is obvious. Absolutely yes!

Out of all the people of history, God chose Abraham. When it came to the fulfillment of His covenant promise, He chose Isaac over Ishmael. Before Isaac's twin sons were born, He chose Jacob over Esau to be His heir of the covenant commitment to Abraham.

God chose Israel over Egypt, Assyria, Babylon, Persia, Greece, Rome, America, and all the other kingdoms of the earth to be His specially chosen people.

God's Word speaks to this when He makes one of the most troubling statements in all of Scripture, "Just as it is written, 'JACOB I LOVED, BUT ESAU I HATED'" (Romans 9:13). Nothing God says in His Word at first reading could seem more unjust. When we think about the original character of Jacob as a lying, scheming mama's boy compared to his outdoorsman brother, it is especially hard to take. Yet we are even more troubled from what seems to be God's injustice in that statement, which the apostle Paul quoted from the Old Testament prophet Malachi.

This Old Testament passage is even tougher to take. The oracle of the word of the Lord to Israel through Malachi:

> "I have loved you," says the LORD. But you say, "How have You loved us?"
>
> "Was not Esau Jacob's brother?" declares the LORD. "Yet I have loved Jacob; but I have hated Esau, and I have made his mountains a desolation and appointed his inheritance for the jackals of the wilderness." Though Edom says, "We have been beaten down, but we will return and build up the ruins"; thus says the LORD of hosts, "They may build, but I will tear down; and men will call them the wicked territory, and the people toward whom the LORD is indignant forever." Your eyes will see this and you will say, "The LORD be magnified beyond the border of Israel" (Malachi 1:2–5).

Here God doesn't just include His favoritism of Jacob over Esau but spreads His condemnation to Esau's heirs, the Edomites. He describes Esau and the Edomites as classic self-reliant men. They have an admirable quality that, when beaten down, they get back up. Any coach would love this in one of his players. Most Americans love this when people who get knocked down (through their own fault or the fault of others) make a comeback. Yet the whole spirit of Edom's self-reliance leaves out God. God is clear. He will use Esau and the Edomites as classic examples that "everyone is good for something if only to serve as a bad example."[1] Scripture is absolutely clear: God does play favorites.

QUESTION #2: IS GOD UNFAIR?

If God plays favorites, then does that mean God is unfair? Scripture is emphatic that the answer is absolutely not. This bewildering answer begins to be explained in God's Word in the very same biblical text where we found the answer to the first question. Romans 9:13 is followed with a question and answer concerning God's justice. "What shall we say then? There is no injustice with God, is there? May it never be!" (Romans 9:14). God's Word answers emphatically: No! God is not unjust. Then God's Word goes on to explain why.

> For He says to Moses, "I WILL HAVE MERCY ON WHOM I HAVE MERCY, AND I WILL HAVE COMPASSION ON WHOM I HAVE COMPASSION." So then it does not depend on the man who wills or the man who runs, but on God who has mercy. For the Scripture says to Pharaoh, "FOR THIS VERY PURPOSE I RAISED YOU UP, TO DEMONSTRATE MY POWER IN YOU, AND THAT MY NAME MIGHT BE PROCLAIMED THROUGHOUT THE WHOLE EARTH." So then He has mercy on whom He desires, and He hardens whom He desires. (Romans 9:15–18)

Because He is God, He can choose to have mercy on whom He wants to have mercy. Whom God chooses has nothing to do with man. In other words, no one is good enough to earn God's favor. "For all have sinned and fall short of the glory of God" or God's perfect plan for our lives (Romans 3:23).

Yes, what the Bible says about Pharaoh reads like determinism. It makes it seem as though people have no choice, to which some hyper-Calvinists would likely agree. But God is just, and He can do what He wants with His creation for His purposes to advance His plan and will for history.

Yet God is patient with all men who are enslaved to sin. Think how patient He was with hard-hearted Pharaoh. He sent Pharaoh nine plagues to get him to change his heart and let God's people go. It wasn't until the tenth plague that God brought His judgment of death on Pharaoh's and the Egyptians' households.

But does this mean Pharaoh had no choice? I do not believe that is the case. That is determinism (God's determining every decision we make), which is very different from God's foreknowledge. God's Word teaches foreknowledge, not determinism. Because God knows all, He knows exactly how we will respond in every situation. He knew Pharaoh's heart would get harder and harder with every new plague. So yes, God hardened his heart, but Pharaoh still had the free will to repent or become more hardened.

At the same time, God can have mercy with whomever He wants. Mercy is something we don't deserve. Abraham, Isaac, Jacob, and the nation of Israel received that grace in being chosen. Everyone who has received Christ in the future receives the grace and mercy of God, though we have done nothing to deserve it. We simply receive the unmerited favor of God we don't deserve.

So is it unfair that God chose Jacob over Esau? Absolutely not. Neither of them deserved to be chosen—especially Jacob. None of us does.

Yet God also knows that many people He loves, like Ishmael and Esau, will continually leave God out. He knows that many, like their heirs, will blame the God of Abraham, Isaac, and Jacob for their troubles and in the process resent and even hate those for whom God has chosen to have mercy. He knows there will always be contempt and resentment to all of us Gentiles whom God has chosen to be His children through receiving in the faith the gospel of Jesus Christ.

QUESTION #3: SO IS THE MIDDLE EAST CONFLICT GOD'S FAULT?

We come to one final question: Is the Middle East conflict God's fault? No, it is man's fault. The origin of the Middle East conflict began with one man's sin—Abraham. Yet the ongoing conflict in the Middle East continues because from the seed of Abraham came the seeds of turmoil, and many today continue to refuse what God offers to everyone—His amazing grace. That is true for heirs of Isaac and Ishmael, Esau and Jacob. It is true for all mankind. For those who refuse God's grace or even worse, refuse to believe they need God's grace, there will be a spirit of arrogance and resentment with God that cries, "It is not fair!" The natural out-growth of this mind-set is anger, bitterness, resentment, hatred, killing, revenge, war, and never-ending evil. This is what has happened with the Middle East conflict. It continues to this very day.

The ultimate hope is found in the grace God offers through His Son, Jesus Christ. This is available to all—Jews, Arabs, Gentiles. God's Word makes this absolutely clear in the very next chapter of Romans. Romans 10:13 says, "WHOEVER WILL CALL ON THE NAME OF THE LORD WILL BE SAVED." *Whoever* includes everyone. That's the ultimate in fairness. God's grace is offered to all.

If you are one of those "whoevers" who needs to call on the name of the Lord to be saved, I hope you will.

Everyone who receives His grace begins a transformation that changes a heart of bitterness and revenge into a heart of grace that forgives those who killed their brothers and loves those who are their enemies. For those who do this in the Middle East, the conflict ends—one life at a time. The seeds of turmoil are transformed into the seeds of love, forgiveness, and peace. Yet because most will not, the cycle of hatred and violence will never end until the Prince of Peace invades history in person once again.

Timeline

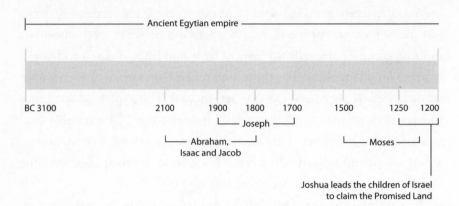

|——————— Ancient Egytian empire ————————————|

BC 3100   2100   1900   1800   1700   1500   1250 1200

└—— Joseph ——┘

└—— Abraham, ——┘
Isaac and Jacob

└—— Moses ——┘

Joshua leads the children of Israel
to claim the Promised Land

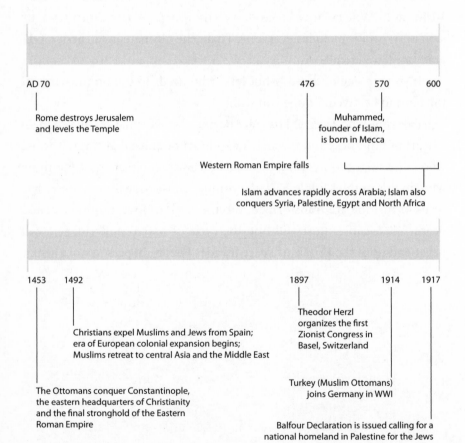

AD 70   476   570   600

Rome destroys Jerusalem
and levels the Temple

Muhammed,
founder of Islam,
is born in Mecca

Western Roman Empire falls

Islam advances rapidly across Arabia; Islam also
conquers Syria, Palestine, Egypt and North Africa

1453   1492   1897   1914   1917

Theodor Herzl
organizes the first
Zionist Congress in
Basel, Switzerland

Christians expel Muslims and Jews from Spain;
era of European colonial expansion begins;
Muslims retreat to central Asia and the Middle East

Turkey (Muslim Ottomans)
joins Germany in WWI

The Ottomans conquer Constantinople,
the eastern headquarters of Christianity
and the final stronghold of the Eastern
Roman Empire

Balfour Declaration is issued calling for a
national homeland in Palestine for the Jews

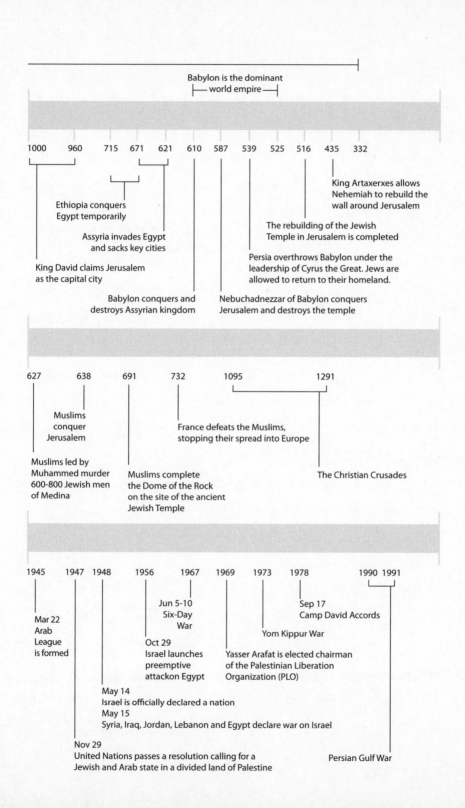

Babylon is the dominant
├── world empire ──┤

| 1000 | 960 | 715 | 671 | 621 | 610 | 587 | 539 | 525 | 516 | 435 | 332 |

King Artaxerxes allows
Nehemiah to rebuild the
wall around Jerusalem

The rebuilding of the Jewish
Temple in Jerusalem is completed

Ethiopia conquers
Egypt temporarily

Persia overthrows Babylon under the
leadership of Cyrus the Great. Jews are
allowed to return to their homeland.

Assyria invades Egypt
and sacks key cities

King David claims Jerusalem
as the capital city

Babylon conquers and
destroys Assyrian kingdom

Nebuchadnezzar of Babylon conquers
Jerusalem and destroys the temple

| 627 | 638 | 691 | 732 | 1095 | 1291 |

Muslims
conquer
Jerusalem

France defeats the Muslims,
stopping their spread into Europe

Muslims led by
Muhammed murder
600-800 Jewish men
of Medina

Muslims complete
the Dome of the Rock
on the site of the ancient
Jewish Temple

The Christian Crusades

| 1945 | 1947 | 1948 | 1956 | 1967 | 1969 | 1973 | 1978 | 1990 | 1991 |

Jun 5-10
Six-Day
War

Sep 17
Camp David Accords

Mar 22
Arab
League
is formed

Yom Kippur War

Oct 29
Israel launches
preemptive
attackon Egypt

Yasser Arafat is elected chairman
of the Palestinian Liberation
Organization (PLO)

May 14
Israel is officially declared a nation
May 15
Syria, Iraq, Jordan, Lebanon and Egypt declare war on Israel

Nov 29
United Nations passes a resolution calling for a
Jewish and Arab state in a divided land of Palestine

Persian Gulf War

GLOSSARY

Abed-nego: Babylonian name of Azariah; a Jewish leader in Babylon whom God delivered from the fiery furnace with Shadrach and Meshach

Abel: the second son of Adam and Eve, who was murdered by his brother, Cain

Abraham: called by God to inherit the promised land of Canaan and promised he would father a vast nation; father of Ishmael by his wife's maid, Hagar; and father of Isaac, the covenant child, by his wife, Sarah; considered the father of Judaism, Christianity, and Islam

Abram: original name of Abraham before God renamed him

Ahasuerus: Hebrew name for King Xerxes

Ahmadinejad, Mahmoud: the sixth and current (2010) president of Iran, a controversial leader and outspoken hater of Israel

Allah: the Arabic name for God, yet character traits in Qur'an are different from the true God of the Bible

Amorites: one of the people groups who inhabited the land promised to the heirs of Abraham

Arab League: an organization of Arabic-speaking nations, including Algeria, Bahrain, Comoros, Djibouti, Egypt, Iraq, Jordan, Kuwait, Lebanon, Libya, Mauritania, Morocco, Oman, Palestine, Qatar, Saudi Arabia, Somalia, Sudan, Syria, Tunisia, United Arab Emirates, and Yemen; established on March 22, 1945, to promote cultural, economic, military, political, and social cooperation

Arab Quarter: one of the four quarters of the ancient walled city of Jerusalem

Arabs: descendants of Ishmael who mostly settled in the Arabian peninsula

Arafat, Yasser: (1929–2004) became leader of the Palestine Liberation Organization (PLO) in 1969; elected in 1996 as the first president of the Palestinian Authority, the newly formed Palestinian self-rule government; shared the 1994 Nobel Peace Prize[1]

Artaxerxes: Persian king who allowed Nehemiah to rebuild the wall around Jerusalem around 435 BC

Assyria: a nation in northern Mesopotamia in Old Testament times; became a large empire during the period of the Israelite kings; Assyrian expansion into the region of Palestine (about 855–625 BC) enormously impacted the Hebrew kingdoms of Israel and Judah[2]

Bedouin Arabs: members of a nomadic tribe of Arabs

Belshazzar: ancient Babylonian king, successor of King Nebuchadnezzar; Daniel interpreted his dream and prophesied that Belshazzar's kingdom would be overthrown by the Medo-Persian empire

Ben-Gurion, David: first prime minister of Israel; instrumental in the founding and building of the Israeli nation

Bethlehem: the birthplace of Jesus Christ, located about five miles southwest of Jerusalem

Bethuel: father of Rebekah, Isaac's wife

Bin Laden, Osama: leader of the terrorist organization al-Qaeda

Cain: first son of Adam and Eve, murdered his brother, Abel

Camp David Accords: peace agreements signed by Egyptian president Anwar El Sadat and Israeli prime minister Menachem Begin on September 17, 1978; the Accords led directly to the 1979 Israel-Egypt Peace Treaty

Canaan: the promised land God promised to Abraham's heirs

Canaanites: one of the people groups who inhabited the land promised to the heirs of Abraham

Churchill, Winston: British politician who served two terms as prime

, minister, most notably during WWII; as a young war minister he led the process of dividing up the Middle Eastern territory following WWI

Constantinople: one of the two most important centers for the early Christian church; modern-day Istanbul

Cush: mostly modern-day Ethiopia

Cyrus the Great: leader of Persia who overthrew Babylon in 539 BC; let the Jews return to their homeland and begin rebuilding the temple

Daniel: Jewish prophet who rose to great leadership in Babylonian and Medo-Persian Empires; he was protected by God when thrown into the lions' den

Darius the Great: Persian leader who ordered the rebuilding of the Jewish temple to continue; temple completed under his reign in 516 BC

Daughters of Heth: a pagan people group who resided in Canaan during the era of the Patriarchs

David: second king of Israel, who followed Saul and preceded Solomon; the first king to unite Israel and Judah and the first to receive the promise of a royal messiah in his line; pictured as the ideal king of God's people, David ruled from about 1005 to 965 BC[3]

Dome of the Rock: Islamic shrine located on the Temple Mount in Jerusalem, over the site of the Second Jewish Temple, the place where legend says Muhammed ascended to heaven

Edomites: heirs of Esau, mostly settled in modern-day Jordan

Egypt: one of the four Arab nations surrounding Israel; site of an ancient civilization that dated from 3100–332 BC

el-Kabir River: river in modern-day Lebanon that some biblical scholars believe to be the northern boundary of the promised land as described in Genesis 15:18

Ephron: the Hittite man from whom Abraham bought the ground for the burial of Sarah; the first purchase of land in the promised land

Esau: first son of Isaac and Rebekah; the older twin brother of Jacob

Esther: Jewish girl who was chosen by King Ahasuerus to be queen; risked death to reveal Haman's plot to destroy the Jews

Euphrates River: river in modern-day Iraq that most believe is the northeastern boundary of the promised land described in Genesis 15:18

Gaza Strip: strip of land between the Mediterranean Sea and Israel; the ancient homeland of the Philistines and presently controlled by the Palestinians

Girgushites: one of the people groups who inhabited the land promised to the heirs of Abraham

Golan Heights: land along the Syrian and Israeli border that is in dispute between the two nations

Gulf of Aqaba: an arm of the Red Sea between the Sinai Peninsula and northwest Saudi Arabia[4]

Hagar: Egyptian maid of Sarah and the mother of Ishmael

Haman: prime minister under the Persian king Ahasuerus who devised a plot to exterminate the Jews

Haran: ancient city of Mesopotamia in modern-day southeast Turkey; the home of Abraham's relative Laban and the place where Jacob was married

Havilah: a geographic region located in some part of north or northeast Arabia; perhaps identified with the sandy tract that skirts Babylonia along the whole of its western border, stretching from the lower Euphrates to the mountains of Edom[5]

Hebron: city in the hill country of Judah, nineteen miles south of Jerusalem; Abraham, who purchased land there to bury Sarah, was also buried there along with Isaac and Rebekah and Jacob and Leah[6]

Herod: king of Judea under the Roman authority when Jesus was born in Bethlehem (Matthew 2:1); received the wise men and sent them on to the Christ child with orders to return to him and let him know where he could find the newly born "King of the Jews;" gave orders to kill the babies of Bethlehem, two years old and younger, in hopes of getting this One whom he saw as a successor to his throne[7]

Herzl, Theodor: Hungarian-born Austrian founder of Zionism; as a correspondent during the Alfred Dreyfus affair, he determined that the solution to anti-Semitism was the establishment of a Jewish national state; founded the Zionist World Congress in 1897[8]

Hittites and Hevites: also known as the "children of Heth"; inhabitants of the land promised to the heirs of Abraham; non-Semitic minorities within the population of Canaan who frequently became involved in the affairs of the Israelites[9]

Holy Land: the region referred to in the Bible as the promised land or Canaan; this area and many sites within it hold significant religious importance to Judaism, Christianity, and Islam

Hussein, Saddam: president of Iraq from 1979 to 2003; in power during the Persian Gulf War of 1991

Iran: an Islamic nation in western Asia; known in the ancient world as Persia

Iraq: an Islamic nation bordering Iran, Syria, Turkey, Jordan, Saudi Arabia, and Kuwait and occupying a great portion of the land of ancient Babylon.

Isaac: covenant child of Abraham and Sarah; married Rebekah and fathered Jacob and Esau

Isaiah: ancient Jewish prophet who prophesied concerning Cyrus the Great

Ishmael: first son of Abraham by Sarah's maid, Hagar

Israel: means "God prevails" or "striving with God"; the name God gave to Jacob; modern-day official state and homeland of the Jewish people

Jacob: original ancestor of the nation of Israel; father of the twelve ancestors of the twelve tribes of Israel; son of Isaac and Rebekah, younger twin brother of Esau, and husband of Leah and Rachel; God changed his name to Israel[10]

Jebusites: inhabitants of the land around Jerusalem that David conquered in 1004 BC

Jerusalem: the capital city of Israel that King David conquered and claimed in 1004 BC; today it is considered a holy city to Jews, Muslims, and Christians and remains highly disputed

Jewish Quarter: the Old City [of Jerusalem], divided into four neighborhoods and named according to the ethnic affiliation of most of the people who live in them; the dividing lines are the street that runs from Damascus Gate to Zion Gate, which divides the city into east and west, and the street leading from Jaffa Gate to Lion's Gate—which bifurcates the city north and south; entering through the Jaffa Gate and traveling to David Street, the Christian Quarter is on the left; continuing down David Street, the Armenian Quarter is on the right; to the left of Jews Street is the Muslim Quarter and to the right is the Jewish Quarter[11]

Jonah: ancient Jewish prophet called by God to preach to the Assyrians of Nineveh

Jordan: an Arab country of southwest Asia in northwest Arabia; inhabited since biblical times, the area was conquered by the Romans (first century AD), Arabs (seventh century), and Ottoman Turks, who held it from 1516 until World War I; as Transjordan, the country became part of the British mandate of Palestine in 1920, gaining independence in 1946; renamed Jordan in 1949 after acquiring the West Bank, which it later renounced in 1974[12]

Joseph: one of the sons of Israel; the eleventh of twelve sons, the first by Jacob's favorite wife, Rachel[13]

Joshua: successor of Moses as leader of ancient Israel; the sixth book of the Bible

Judaism: the religion of the Israelites of the Bible and of the Jews of today, based on the teachings of the Torah; involves the belief in one God, whose chosen people are the Jews; Abraham is considered the founder of Judaism although Moses, who delivered the laws of God to the Israelites, is also an important figure[14]

Kadesh-barnea: place name meaning "consecrated"; the site where the Hebrews stayed for most of thirty-eight years after leaving Mount Sinai and before entering the promised land[15]

Kadmonites: one of the people groups who inhabited the land promised to the heirs of Abraham

Kenites: one of the people groups who inhabited the land promised to the heirs of Abraham

Kenizzites: one of the people groups who inhabited the land promised to the heirs of Abraham

Khan, Genghis: Mongolian general and emperor of the late twelfth and early thirteenth centuries; known for his military leadership and great cruelty; conquered vast portions of northern China and southwestern Asia[16]

Khomeini, Ayatollah: (1900–1989) a supreme religious leader in the Iranian Shiite Muslim community; on February 11, 1979, his revolutionary forces seized power in Iran, and he emerged as the leader of the Islamic Republic of Iran[17]

Laban: Rebekah's brother and the father of Leah and Rachel (Genesis 29:16)[18]

Leah: oldest daughter of Laban; first wife of Jacob

Lebanon: an Arab nation at the east end of the Mediterranean Sea, on the northern border of Israel

Lot: Abraham's nephew

Luther, Martin: Catholic monk who protested corruption in the church and called for reform

Mao Tse-tung: Chinese revolutionary leader of the twentieth century; in 1949 his armies took over the country and established the People's Republic of China; Mao continued as chairman of China's Communist party and as premier[19]

Marduk: the Persian god of Zoroastrianism

Marxism: the doctrines of Karl Marx and his associate Friedrich Engels on economics, politics, and society, including the notion of economic determinism—political and social structures are determined by the economic conditions of people; Marxism calls for a classless society in which all means of production are commonly owned (communism), a system to be reached as an inevitable result of the struggle between the leaders of capitalism and the workers[20]

Mecca: city of western Saudi Arabia near the coast of the Red Sea; birthplace of Muhammad, considered the holiest city of Islam and a pilgrimage site for all devout believers of the faith[21]

Medina: city of western Saudi Arabia, north of Mecca; the Mosque of the Prophet, containing Muhammad's tomb, a holy site for Muslim pilgrims, is located here[22]

Medo-Persian Empire: dominant world empire after Babylon

Meshach: Babylonian name of Mishael—Jewish leader in Babylon who survived the fiery furnace

Middle East: the countries of southwest Asia and northeast Africa lying west of Afghanistan, Pakistan, and India; thus defined, it includes Cyprus, the Asian part of Turkey, Syria, Lebanon, Israel, the West Bank and Gaza, Jordan, Iraq, Iran, the countries of the Arabian peninsula (Saudi Arabia, Yemen, Oman, United Arab Emirates, Qatar, Bahrain, and Kuwait), and Egypt and Libya[23]

Mordecai: Esther's cousin and the mastermind behind her rise to power and subsequent victory over the evil Haman[24]

Moses: leader of the Israelites in their exodus from Egyptian slavery and oppression and their journey through the wilderness with its threats in the form of hunger, thirst, and unpredictable enemies; finally their audience with God at Mount Sinai/Horeb where the distinctive covenant, bonding Israel and God in a special treaty, became a reality[25]

Mount Moriah: site of Abraham's willingness to sacrifice Isaac; also the site in Jerusalem where Solomon built the original Jewish temple; now the site of the Dome of the Rock

Muhammad: the founder of Islam in the seventh century AD

Muslims: followers of Allah in the religion of Islam

Nasser, Abdul: Egyptian army officer and politician who served as prime minister (1954–1956) and president (1956–1958) of Egypt and as president of the United Arab Republic (1958–1970); his nationalization of the Suez Canal precipitated an international crisis (1956)[26]

Nazism: the ideology and practice of the Nazis, especially the policy of racist nationalism, national expansion, and state control of the economy[27]

Nebuchadnezzar: king of Babylon who leveled Jerusalem in 587 BC

Nineveh: ancient capital of Assyria

Ottoman Empire: an empire developed by the Turks between the fourteenth and twentieth centuries; succeeded in the 1920s by the present-day republic of Turkey; at its peak the Ottoman Empire included, besides present-day Turkey, large parts of the Middle East and southeastern Europe[28]

Paddan-aram: the land from where Abraham journeyed to Canaan; one of the principal cities was Haran.[29]

Palestine: Roman derivative of "Philistine"; name given to the land of Judea and Jerusalem after Rome destroyed Jerusalem and expelled the Jews

Paul: outstanding missionary and writer to the early church; Paul the apostle and his theology are important in the New Testament, not only because thirteen epistles bear his name but also because of the extended biographical information given in the book of Acts; from these two sources, we piece together a reasonable picture of one of the major personalities of early Christianity[30]

Penuel: place where Jacob wrestled with God

Perizzites: one of the people groups who inhabited the land promised to the heirs of Abraham

Persia: an ancient empire of southwest Asia; the land is now mostly Iran, but the empire was much larger

Persian Gulf War: a war between the forces of the United Nations—led by the United States—and those of Iraq; followed Iraqi dictator Saddam Hussein's invasion of Kuwait in August 1990; UN forces, called the Coalition, expelled Iraqi troops from Kuwait in March 1991[31]

Philistines: longtime enemy of the Israelites, mostly inhabiting what is now the Gaza Strip

Pilate, Pontius: Roman governor of Judea, remembered in history as a notorious anti-Semite and in Christian creeds as the magistrate under whom Jesus Christ "suffered"[32]

PLO: Palestinian Liberation Organization

Qadhafi, Muammar: Libyan political leader who seized power in a military coup d'état against the Libyan monarchy (1969) and imposed socialist policies and Islamic orthodoxy on the country[33]

Qur'an: the Holy Book of Islam

Rachel: second daughter of Laban; second wife of Jacob

Rebekah: wife of Isaac and mother of Esau and Jacob

Rephaimites: one of the people groups who inhabited the land promised to the heirs of Abraham

Rome: one of the two most important centers for the early Christian church; Vatican City, headquarters of the Roman Catholic Church, is in Rome

Samaritans: Jewish half-breeds who had intermarried with Assyrians

Sarah: the name God gave to Abram/Abraham's wife, Sarai

Satraps: nationlike divisions within the vast ancient Persian empire

Saudi Arabia: monarchy occupying most of the Arabian Peninsula, where it is bordered by Jordan, Iraq, and Kuwait to the north; the Persian Gulf, Qatar, and the United Arab Emirates to the east; Oman to the east and south; Yemen to the south; and the Red Sea and the Gulf of Aqaba to the west; its capital and largest city is Riyadh[34]

Saul: first king of Israel

Shadrach: Babylonian name of Hananiah, Jewish leader in Babylon who survived the fiery furnace

Shechem: the site where Abraham built an altar, acknowledging he had arrived in the land God had given him

Shiites: one of the two great divisions of Islam that regards Ali, the son-in-law of Muhammad, and his descendants as the legitimate successors to Muhammad and rejects the first three caliphs who succeeded him[35]

Shur: region on Egypt's northeastern border, perhaps named after the wall Egyptians built to protect their border, where Moses made first stop after crossing the Red Sea (Exodus 15:22); earlier, Sarah's handmaid, Hagar, had come toward Shur after her expulsion from the clan of Abraham (Genesis 16:7)[36]

Sinai Peninsula: peninsula in northeastern Egypt, bordered by the Gulf of Aqaba, an arm of the Red Sea, to the east; and by the Gulf of Suez, another arm of the Red Sea, to the west[37]

Solomon: son of King David and Bathsheba; the third king of Israel

Stalin, Joseph: Soviet politician; the successor of Lenin, general secretary of the Communist Party (1922–1953), and premier of the USSR (1941–1953); his rule was marked by the exile of Trotsky (1929), a purge of the government and military, the forced collectivization of agriculture, a policy of industrialization, and a victorious but devastating role for the Soviets in World War II[38]

Sunnis: one of the two great divisions of Islam that accepts the first four caliphs as rightful successors of Muhammad[39]

Syria: a country of southwest Asia on the eastern Mediterranean coast; ancient Syria also included Lebanon, most of present-day Israel and Jordan, and part of Iraq and Saudi Arabia; settled c. 2100 BC by Amorites, the region was later conquered by Hittites, Assyrians, Babylonians, Persians, Greeks, and Romans; Islam was introduced in the seventh century by Muslim Arab conquerors; Damascus is the capital and Aleppo the largest city[40]

Temple Mount: an elevated plateau in the Old City of Jerusalem, sacred to Jews, Muslims, and Christians; originally the site of the great temple of Jerusalem, the holiest place in Judaism; for Muslims, it is the site of the Prophet Muhammad's journey to heaven, described in the Qur'an; Christians revere it as a place frequently visited by Jesus, and some believe it will play a major role in end-time events[41]

Tigris River: site of the major vision of the prophet Daniel (Daniel 10:4); significant cities located on its banks included Nineveh, the ancient capital of the Assyrian Empire, located on its east bank; and farther south, Asshur, religious center and original capital of Assyria[42]

Transjordan: an area east of the Jordan River in southwest Asia; a British mandate (1921–23); an emirate (1923–49); now the major part of the kingdom of Jordan[43]

Ur: Abraham's home city, which he left to go to the promised land; located in modern-day Iraq

West Bank: a disputed territory of southwest Asia between Israel and Jordan west of the Jordan River; part of Jordan after 1949, it was occupied by Israel in the 1967 Arab-Israeli War; in 1994 an accord between Israel and the PLO was signed, giving Palestinians limited self-rule and requiring measured withdrawal of Israeli troops from the West Bank[44]

Zionism: a Jewish movement that arose in the late nineteenth century in response to growing anti-Semitism; it sought to reestablish a Jewish homeland in Palestine; modern Zionism is concerned with the support and development of the state of Israel[45]

Zoroastrianism: ancient religion of Persia developed between 1400 and 1000 BC; teaches that there is one God over all

STUDY AND DISCUSSION GUIDE

This study and discussion guide was written to help you dig deeper into the topics presented in this book. Whether used for your own personal study or with a group, the following suggestions will deepen your understanding of the material and enhance your reading experience.

- While reading each chapter, make notes in the margins of the book or in a separate journal. Ask questions, mark scriptures, and make a list of topics to investigate. These notes will help you dive deeper into the material.
- After reading each chapter, work through this guide for additional thought-provoking questions, expanded study activities, and prayer prompts.
- Finally, consider sharing your thoughts and insights with a small group. There is nothing like the lively discussion and unique insights that come from studying a book like *Seeds of Turmoil* with others. Select a group leader who will keep the discussion flowing, including everyone who wants to speak, while keeping an eye on the clock so as to start and end on time. Each member should bring his book with margin notes and/or journal and come prepared by having done his homework.

For further insight into the topics presented in this book, please visit us at www.rightfromtheheart.org.

CHAPTER 1

One Man's Decision: Abraham

1. List some important life decisions that people are faced with making. Identify one in your own life and consider how you arrived at a final decision. If enough time has passed for the answer to be evident, would you consider that it was a good or a bad decision? What would you have changed about the process?

2. Waiting on God and His timing is hard. Describe a time in your life when you found it difficult to wait for God's direction. Read Psalm 27:14, Isaiah 30:18, and Isaiah 64:4, and discuss how these verses might prove helpful in making future decisions.

3. If God asks you to wait in a specific situation, does that mean you are to do nothing? What might you consider doing while you wait? What should you *not* do while you wait?

4. What does this chapter show about the power of influence a husband or wife has over his/her spouse? If you are married, what does this mean with regard to your influence? What about how you respond to your spouse's influence?

5. Isaac, not Ishmael, was the "child of promise" given to Abraham and Sarah (Genesis 17:21). How does that strike you about the fairness of God and the consequences of our sin?

6. The word *Ishmael* means "God hears" (Genesis 16:11). Has God heard your prayers in a time of need or desperation? Recall a time God answered your prayers, recount some of the details, and either vocalize or write a prayer of thanksgiving.

7. What is happening today in the Middle East that concerns you the most? Spend a few moments in prayer asking God to bring peace, grace, and His gospel to that troubled region.

Chapter 2

An Everlasting Possession: The Holy Land

1. If you have never visited Israel (and even if you have), visit www .virtualworldproject.org. Click on the sites of Jerusalem, En Gedi, Masada, Capernaum, Bethsaida, and Caesarea, and enjoy high quality, panoramic photos of the Holy Land.

2. When God called Abraham out of Ur (Genesis 12:1), He asked Abraham to take a huge step of faith. Describe a time in your life when God asked you to take a step of faith. How did you respond?

3. Before reading this chapter, what did you know about the ancient history of the Holy Land? What new insights did you gain?

4. After reading this chapter on God's promises concerning the land, how will you view differently news about conflict over the land?

5. The founding of the modern state of Israel (May 14, 1948) is a fascinating study of history. How did you see God's hand at work as you read this chapter?

6. Time and time again in the modern age, God has miraculously protected Israel from attacks by Arab and Muslim armies. What surprised you about the accounts of the 1948 war and the Six-Day War?

7. God's covenant with Abraham concerning his heirs and the land was an everlasting one. What are some other promises or covenants in Scripture that are everlasting? As examples, read Genesis 9:12–16; Isaiah 9:6–7; Isaiah 45:17; John 6:47; and Galatians 3:13–14, 29.

8. Take a few moments and pray for God's protection on Jews living in Israel. Pray for Arab Muslims who have so much understandable bitterness over the land. Pray most of all that they would recognize Jesus Christ as the Messiah.

CHAPTER 3

Two Women Who Shaped History: Sarah and Hagar

1. Infertility in ancient Near Eastern cultures was thought of as a sign of God's judgment, just as having multiple children seemed to indicate God's blessing. Do we have similar "signs" of God's judgment and blessing in our culture today?

2. "God helps those who help themselves" is a famous nonbiblical quote that is often thought of as scripture. Can you think of other popular platitudes and sayings that sound biblical but, in fact, are not?

3. Sarah had to trust God in a faith-stretching way. Has there been a time in your life when you have had to trust God in a seemingly impossible situation? Describe your thoughts and feelings as you moved forward in faith (or perhaps fear). Did any specific scriptures help you along the way (for example, Proverbs 3:5–6)?

4. Why do we often struggle to believe the promises of God? What holds us back?

5. Genesis 16:2 reads, "Abram listened to the voice of Sarai." When it comes to getting advice for your life, whom do you seek out or where do you turn? Do you have trusted counselors who have helped you make decisions? Read the following scriptures:

   Job 12:13
   Psalm 1:1–3
   Psalm 119:24
   Proverbs 12:15
   Proverbs 15:22

Romans 8:26

James 1:5

6. Make note of the theophanies from the Old Testament that were identified in this chapter. How might they cause you to view Jesus differently?

7. Even though God's covenant with Abraham was through Isaac, He still protected and blessed Ishmael and Hagar (Genesis 21:17–19). Why do you think this is the case?

8. If you are a wife or mother, spend some time in prayer, asking God to work powerfully in your life to be a good spiritual and moral influence on your husband and/or child.

CHAPTER 4

Sibling Rivalry: Isaac and Ishmael

1. The sibling rivalry between Ishmael and Isaac was due in part to their birth order—Ishmael first, then Isaac. Research has shown that birth order has differing effects on children. What is your birth order? How do you think this affected your childhood? Your adulthood?

2. Put yourself in sixteen-year-old Ishmael's sandals for a moment. As a teenager, how might you have dealt with that kind of rejection?

3. What is the main insight from this chapter that helps you understand the Middle East conflict today?

4. God's original intent for marriage was "one woman, one man" (Genesis 2:24; Matthew 19:3–6). Unfortunately, this model is becoming rarer and rarer in modern society. What factors do you think are behind the rise in divorce, same-sex marriages, and cohabitation?

5. God kept His promise to Abraham and Sarah concerning Isaac. How has God kept a specific biblical promise to you? Read the following promises found in God's Word:

    Joshua 1:5

    Psalm 1:1–6

    Proverbs 3:5–6

    Matthew 7:7–8

    John 14:15–18

    John 14:27

    Romans 8:35, 37–39

    1 Corinthians 10:13

6. Luke 1:37 states that nothing is impossible with God. Reflect on this truth and discuss how it can change your prayer life. How might it change your daily life?

7. Reread Genesis 22:15–18, where God asked Abraham to sacrifice Isaac. We cannot imagine actually doing this physical act ourselves, but consider that Isaac is symbolic of the things we hold dear. What might God be asking you to consider sacrificing or releasing to Him?

8. Consider if there may be any unresolved issues in your family that need resolution, perhaps with your parents or siblings. Spend a few moments in prayer, asking God to forgive you if you were in error. Pray for reconciliation in your family. Do you need to contact your family members to make things right? If so, follow through quickly.

CHAPTER 5

Playing Favorites: Isaac and Rebekah, Esau and Jacob

1. Have you been on either side of the playing-favorites game? How did it feel? Read Romans 2:11, 1 Timothy 5:21, and James 2:1–9, and discuss how God views playing favorites.

2. Reread the story about Isaac's servant discovering Rebekah, Isaac's future wife (Genesis 24). How can this story serve as an encouragement and example for your prayer life? Have you experienced something similar to this?

3. From the very beginning of Rebekah's pregnancy, God foresaw the future of the two boys (Genesis 25:23). Do you think God saw your future as well? Reflect upon Psalm 139:13–16.

4. Both Esau ("hairy") and Jacob ("deceiver") received names that described them well. So did many other Bible characters, such as Adam ("ground" or "man," Genesis 2:7); Eve ("living," Genesis 3:20); Abraham ("father of many nations," Genesis 17:5); Isaac ("he laughs," Genesis 17:19); and Jesus ("the Lord saves," Matthew 1:21). What is the history or etymology of your name? Did you have a nickname in your childhood?

5. Jacob and Rebekah "cooked up" a scheme to cheat Esau and deceive Isaac (Genesis 27:1–29). Describe a situation when you were cheated or wronged. How did it make you feel? How did you handle the situation? Study the prayer of Jesus in Matthew 6:12–15 for insight into how to deal with people who harm you.

6. When Jacob pretended to be Esau, he lied to his father, Isaac, not once, but four times (Genesis 27:18–24). What happens when

lies are introduced to a situation? How do we face the temptation to manipulate our way into, or out of, circumstances that are difficult or not as we'd like? Consider the wisdom in Exodus 20:16, Leviticus 19:11, and Colossians 3:9.

7. If you are a parent with children in the home, spend some time praying for them. Ask God to show you how to help your children discover and fulfill God's will for their lives, rather than what you want for their lives.

CHAPTER 6

Reaping What You Sow: Jacob and the Birth of Israel

1. Despite all his shortcomings and his troubled past, God chose to bless Jacob. How does this encourage you as you consider your own life's shortcomings and past?

2. Guilt can be "haunting, unshakable glue to the soul," as mentioned in this chapter. Study these verses on guilt and forgiveness: Matthew 26:27–28; Ephesians 1:7–8; Colossians 1:13–14; Hebrews 10:19–22; and 1 John 1:9. What truths do you see? How might they be applied in your own life?

3. Jacob had a remarkable dream in Genesis 28:12–15. In fact, dreams are mentioned throughout the book of Genesis (for example, Genesis 20:3; 31:10–13, 24; 37:5–11; and 40:4–19) and the rest of the Bible (for example, Judges 7:13; 1 Kings 3:5; Daniel 2:1–49; Joel 2:28; Matthew 1:20; Matthew 2:12–22; and Acts 16:9–10). Have you ever had a dream that turned out to be meaningful for the future?

4. God speaks a great promise to Jacob in Genesis 28:15: "Behold, I am with you and will keep you wherever you go." Study these verses and reflect on God's promise to you: Deuteronomy 31:6–8; Psalm 94:14; Matthew 28:20; and John 14:16–17.

5. God used painful lessons in Jacob's life to shape his character. Reflect on a time in your life when God used a painful lesson to shape you. Use Genesis 50:19–20 and Romans 8:28 as points of reference.

6. Jacob wrestled with God in Genesis 32:24–32, a scene described as a "dark night of the soul." Have you experienced something

similar to a "dark night of the soul"? If so, how did your life change after this event?

7. What insights from this chapter did you gain about the West Bank? Jordan? The current Middle East conflict? Spend a few moments praying for the leaders of Middle East countries.

CHAPTER 7

A Miraculous Restoration: The State of Israel and Neighboring Arab Nations

1. Take a moment or two and scan the headlines of your favorite news channel, Web site, or newspaper. How many of the major events of the day involve Israel and the Middle East? How do you think the troubles in that part of the world can be resolved?

2. In this chapter we learned about several ancient kingdoms and their modern-day counterparts. How does it help you better understand those nations today? How long do you think the United States will be the world's most powerful nation? Which nation will follow the United States in that role? Use Proverbs 14:34 as a point of reference.

3. You may have been surprised to learn that the Christian celebration of the Eucharist (the Lord's Supper) has its basis in the Jewish celebration of the Passover. Spend a few moments reflecting on both celebrations (Exodus 12:1–30 and Luke 22:7–23) and note the similarities and the differences.

4. In this chapter, we read the story of Jonah, who was sent on a mission from God to share God's message with a pagan people. Take a few minutes and read this remarkable story in the Old Testament book of Jonah. Is there any part of Jonah's life that you can relate to?

5. Three times in the book of Jeremiah God calls the pagan king Nebuchadnezzar "My servant" (25:9; 27:6; 43:10). Do you find it strange that God would use a pagan king to punish His own people?

6. The story of Daniel's companions defying Nebuchadnezzar is a well-known Bible story (Daniel 3). Have you had a "faith under fire" situation, where you were challenged to stand up for your beliefs? If so, describe what happened and reflect on how God worked through that situation.

7. Jeremiah 29:11–13 has brought hope and encouragement to believers for centuries. Read these verses, and reflect on how God's promise to the people of Israel can be an encouragement to you as well.

8. In light of Jeremiah 29:14, spend some time praying the key line of the Lord's Prayer in Matthew 6:10, knowing that all this is in preparation for Jesus' second coming: "Your kingdom come. Your will be done, on earth as it is in heaven."

CHAPTER 8

Israel's Greatest Threat Today: Iran

1. Given the current Middle East crisis, were you surprised to read that Persia was once favorably disposed toward Israel? Read Genesis 12:3 and Exodus 3:21; 11:3; and 12:36. How has God been "favorably disposed" toward you?

2. One of the unique attributes of the Bible is its amazing prophetic accuracy. Isaiah's prophecy about Cyrus (Isaiah 44:28) is but one example. Study these others and note the predictive power of the Bible: Micah 5:1–2 (the city of the Messiah's birth); Jeremiah 31:15 (the slaughter of the Bethlehem children); Isaiah 35:5–6 (the Messiah would do miracles); Zechariah 9:9 (Palm Sunday); Isaiah 53:1–3 (the rejection of the Messiah by the people); Psalm 22 (the crucifixion of the Messiah); and Psalm 16:8–11 (the resurrection of the Messiah).

3. God used the faith of Daniel to turn King Nebuchadnezzar and King Darius toward God. Whom has God used in your life to turn you toward God?

4. Read the book of Esther in the Old Testament. Note how often the main characters, Esther and Mordecai, had to depend on God despite seemingly impossible circumstances.

5. Haman, Hitler, and now Ahmadinejad have sought to destroy the Jewish people, yet God continues to spare His people and bless them. Why do you think this is so?

6. What do you think God has in mind for you "for such a time as this" (Esther 4:14)? Do you have a sense of a divine mission?

Read Matthew 22:36–40; Matthew 28:18–20; and 2 Corinthians 5:16–21 for insight.

7. What can you learn about seeking the heart of God from the examples of Esther and Mordecai? See Esther 4:1–3 and 4:16–17.

8. Take a moment to thank God for being in charge of all of human history. Pray that the nations would turn to Him and repent of their ungodly ways. Use Psalm 67 as a guide.

CHAPTER 9

The Jewish Perspective

1. Mount Moriah in Jerusalem—home of the Temple Mount and location of the Dome of the Rock—is a holy site to both Jews and Muslims. Some Jews have definitive plans to rebuild the third temple on a site near (or on top of) the Dome of the Rock. How do you think this real estate dilemma will be resolved, if at all?

2. How can a Jewish background inform and enhance Christian doctrine and worship? Study the following verses in the book of Hebrews for insight: 4:14–16; 9:11–28; 10:1–25; 13:11–15.

3. Review the Ten Commandments list from this chapter, or in Exodus 20:1–17. Is it possible to keep these commandments in our society today? Which commandment is hardest for you to keep?

4. The Jews are blessed with a rich faith story from their ancestors (Abraham, Isaac, and Jacob). What is the faith story of your family (if any)? Consider the faith story that you are even now passing along to those who will come after you.

5. Imagine for a moment that you are a Jew living in first-century Jerusalem. How do you think you would have responded to the ministry and teachings of Jesus? With skepticism? Doubt? Anger? Belief?

6. Jesus is the centerpiece of Christianity, but He is also central to the "completion" of the Jewish faith. Why do you think so few Jews have believed in Jesus (Romans 11)? Study the apostle Peter's appeal to Jews to believe in Jesus as Messiah in Acts 2:14–41.

7. How do you think nonbelievers in your community view Jesus? Review Acts 4:12 and then spend a few moments praying that nonbelievers would trust Jesus as their Savior and Messiah.

CHAPTER 10

The Islamic Perspective

1. What new insights did you gain from this chapter about: Muhammad's early life? His early vision for Islam? The later developments of Islam?

2. Review the quotes in this chapter from the Qur'an about the Jews (Sura 5:82 and Sura 98:6). How can these passages help you better understand the conflict between Jews and Muslims?

3. Islam spread rapidly in the Middle East, North Africa, and in parts of Europe between AD 622 and 1492. As you read about this history, what surprised you about the spread of Islam?

4. In this chapter, we read about Islam's desire for worldwide submission to Allah. How does Islam's vision for "evangelism" and conversion of unbelievers compare to and differ from Christianity's? See John 1:10–13; 1 Corinthians 13:4–8; 2 Corinthians 5:16–21; and 1 Peter 3:15.

5. What are the fundamental differences between Islam, Christianity, and Judaism? For more insight, go to the North American Mission Board's Web site, www.4truth.net, and access "world religions."

6. Reflect for a moment on Israel's miraculous military victories in 1948, 1956, 1967, and 1973. Why do you think God continues to bless Israel, despite the fact that most of the country is secular and has rejected Jesus as the true Messiah? See the apostle Paul's discussion about Israel in Romans 9–11 for additional insight.

7. We read almost daily about the conflict between Shiite and Sunni Muslims in the Middle East. Christianity has also struggled with

divisions over the centuries. In your opinion, what divisions within Christianity were needed? What divisions were needless?

8. How has the prophecy of Genesis 16:12 been fulfilled in our world through today? How does this guide you in praying for the heirs of Ishmael to come to faith in Christ?

CHAPTER 11

The Christian Perspective

1. How much do you know about the life, ministry, and teachings of Jesus? Take a moment to study these key events in Jesus' life:

   Events surrounding His birth (Matthew 1:18–2:23)

   Miracles He performed (Matthew 4:23–24; 8:1–17; 8:23–9:12; 9:18–34)

   His longer sermons (Matthew 5–7; 10–13; 18–20; 23–25)

   The names of His twelve disciples (Matthew 10:2–4)

   Groups that opposed Jesus (Matthew 12:38; 15:1–2; 16:1; 21:15; 21:45)

   Events surrounding the last week of His life (Matthew 21–26)

   Events on the day of His crucifixion (Matthew 27)

   Events on the day of His resurrection (Matthew 28:1–15)

   Events after His resurrection (Matthew 28:16–20)

2. How did you feel as you read the description of modern-day Bethlehem in light of what happened in Bethlehem after Jesus' birth there (Matthew 2:13–23)?

3. Study Revelation 12:1–9, and review the discussion of these verses in this chapter. What (if anything) have you been taught about these verses? How do you interpret these verses?

4. Whether on your own or with a group: pray for the peace of Jerusalem (Psalm 122:6–9); recommit (or commit for the first time) to love Jesus and follow His teachings (Matthew 22:37–39); and pray for the imminent return of Jesus (Revelation 22:20–21).

SOME FINAL THOUGHTS

Three Burning Guestions

1. Answer the questions posed in this chapter in your own words: Does God play favorites? Is God unfair? Is the Middle East conflict God's fault?
2. Having read this book, how do you now feel about the Middle East situation? More hopeful? Less hopeful? What were the big takeaways for your own life?
3. Consider adding this prayer to your list of daily prayer concerns: that Jews, Arabs, and Christians would come to the peace that can only be found in Jesus.

Notes

Chapter 1: One Man's Decision

1. Zig Ziglar, *Confessions of a Happy Christian* (New York: Pelican, 1980), 21.
2. Gene Veith, "What If the Muslims Won?" *Tabletalk*, July 1, 2008, http://www.ligonier.org/learn/articles/what-if-muslims-won/ (accessed February 16, 2010).
3. William Lane Craig, *The Only Wise God* (Eugene, OR: Wipf and Stock Publishers, 1999), 127.
4. David Van Biema, "The Legacy of Abraham: Muslims, Christians and Jews All Claim Him as Their Father," *Time*, September 30, 2002, http://www.time.com/time/magazine/article/0,9171,1003355,00.html (accessed February 16, 2010).
5. While some biblical events occurred while their names were Abram and Sarai (before God changed their names), in this book I refer to them as Abraham and Sarah for consistency.
6. Edward E. Hindson and Woodrow Michael Kroll, ed., *Liberty Commentary Bible* (Nashville, TN: Thomas Nelson, 1994), 50.
7. Ernest Jones, *The Life and Work of Sigmund Freud* (New York: Basic Books, Inc., 1961), 377.
8. Kenneth A. Matthews, ed., *NAC Commentary*, vol. 1b (Nashville, TN: B&H Publishers, 1996), 363.
9. *World Book Encyclopedia*, s.v. "Arabian Peninsula."
10. Henry Morris, *The Genesis Record* (Grand Rapids, MI: Baker House Books, 1976), 410.
11. Josephus, *Antiquities of the Jews*, bk. 1, chap. 12.4.

Chapter 2: An Everlasting Possession

1. R. Steven Notley and Anson F. Rainey, *The Sacred Bridge: Carta's Atlas of the Biblical World* (Jerusalem: Carta, 2005), 9.

2. Ibid.

3. *World Book Encyclopedia*, s.v. "Balfour Declaration."

4. Donald Wagner, "Christians and Zion: British Stirrings," *Daily Star*, October 9, 2003, http://www.informationclearinghouse.info/article4959 .htm (accessed November 20, 2009).

5. Paul Johnson, *History of the Jews* (New York: Harper Perennial, 1987), 428.

6. Ibid., 427–28.

7. "Jewish and Non-Jewish Population of Palestine-Israel," The Jewish Virtual Library, http://www.jewishvirtuallibrary.org/jsource/Society_&_Culture/ israel_palestine_pop.html (accessed February 16, 2010).

8. UN General Assembly, Second Session, Official Records, *Resolution 181 (II). Future government of Palestine*, November 29, 1947, http://unispal .un.org/unispal.nsf/0/7F0AF2BD897689B785256C330061D253 (accessed January 25, 2010).

9. For more details of this internal struggle, read David Jeremiah, *What in the World Is Going On?* (Nashville, TN: Thomas Nelson, 2008).

10. David Jeremiah, *What in the World Is Going On?* (Nashville, TN: Thomas Nelson, 2008), 21.

11. Commonly attributed to Abdul Nasser.

12. Jeremiah, *What in the World Is Going On?*, 20.

13. US Central Intelligence Agency, "The Consequences of the Partition of Palestine," November 28, 1947, http://www.foia.cia.gov/browse_docs_full .asp (accessed January 27, 2010).

14. The Palestine National Charter, July 17, 1968, http://avalon.law.yale .edu/20th_century/plocov.asp#art1 (accessed February 16, 2010).

15. Ibid.

16. Arnold Fruchtenbaum, e-mail message to author, November 24, 2008.

17. Notley and Rainey, *The Sacred Bridge*, 34.

Chapter 3: Two Women Who Shaped History

1. Benjamin Franklin, *Poor Richard's Almanac* (New York: The Century Co., 1898), 42.

2. Tom Kelly and Ben Clerkin, "The British Woman Who Became the World's Oldest Natural Mother at 59," *Mail Online*, http://www.dailymail .co.uk/news/article-476452/The-British-woman-worlds-oldest-natural-mother-59.html (accessed February 16, 2010).

3. David Zinman, "A Century of Strom Thurmond," *Atlanta Journal Constitution*, December 2, 2002.

4. The Declaration of Independence of the United States of America.

Chapter 4: Sibling Rivalry

1. Tom Elliff, "Kingdom Families . . .The Importance of Deciding Now!" *SBC Life*, June/July 2004.
2. Edward E. Hindson and Woodrow Michael Kroll, ed., *Liberty Commentary Bible* (Nashville, TN: Thomas Nelson, 1994), 68.
3. Gerhard Von Rad, *Genesis: A Commentary* (Philadelphia, PA: Westminster Press, 1961), 232.

Chapter 5: Playing Favorites

1. William Manchester, *The American Caesar* (Boston, MA: Little, Brown and Company, 1978), 4.

Chapter 6: Reaping What You Sow

1. Trent C. Butler, ed., *Holman Bible Dictionary* (Nashville, TN: Holman Bible Publishers, 1991), s.v. "Israel," 722.
2. Catherine Herridge, "Obama's Apparent Bow to Saudi King Outrages Conservatives," Fox News, April 10, 2009, http://www.foxnews.com/ politics/2009/04/10/obamas-apparent-bow-saudi-king-outrages-conservatives (accessed February 16, 2010).
3. Thomas V. Brisco, *Holman Bible Atlas* (Nashville, TN: B&H Publishing Group, 1998), 73.
4. Shimon Apisdorf, *Judaism in a Nutshell: Israel* (Rochester, NY: Leviathan Press, 2002), 57.
5. Ibid.

Chapter 7: A Miraculous Restoration

1. Trent C. Butler, ed., *Holman Bible Dictionary* (Nashville, TN: Holman Bible Publishers, 1991), s.v. "Hittites and Hevites," 655, 658.
2. Ibid., s.v. "Egypt," 402.
3. Ibid., s.v. "Assyria," 124.

Chapter 8: Israel's Greatest Threat Today

1. Ewan MacAskill and Chris McGreal, "Israel Should Be Wiped Off Map, Says Iran's President," *Guardian*, October 27, 2005, http://www.guardian .co.uk/world/2005/oct/27/israel.iran (accessed February 17, 2010).
2. Trent C. Butler, ed., *Holman Bible Dictionary* (Nashville, TN: Holman Bible Publishers, 1991), s.v. "Persia," 1097–98.
3. Josephus, *Antiquities of the Jews*, bk. 11, chap. 1.1–1.2.

4. Butler, *Holman Bible Dictionary*, s.v. "Cyrus," 328.
5. Paul Johnson, *History of the Jews* (New York, NY: Harper Perennial, 1987), 85.
6. W. D. Davies and Louis Finkelstein, ed., *The Cambridge History of Judaism*, vol. 1 (Cambridge, UK: Cambridge University Press, 1984), 280–83.

Chapter 9: The Jewish Perspective

1. When the Catholic monk Martin Luther protested corruption in the church, he called for the church to return to Scripture alone as its authority (*solo scriptura*). Since the Apocrypha was never considered Scripture, it is not contained in the Bible that Protestants use, which consists of the Old Testament and New Testament only.
2. Uriya Shavit, "Jews, Muslims and the Nobel Prize," August 13, 2009, http://www.adelsoninstitute.org.il/PointOfView.aspx?id=70 (accessed February 17, 2010).

Chapter 10: The Islamic Perspective

1. Emir Fethi Caner and Ergun Mehmet Caner, *Unveiling Islam: An Insider's Look at Muslim Life and Beliefs* (Grand Rapids, MI: Kregel Publications, 2009), 83.
2. Ibid., 39.
3 Ibid., 39–40.
4. Ibid., 40.
5. Karen Armstrong, *Islam, a Short History* (New York: The Modern Library, 2000), 22.
6. Efraim Karsh, *Islamic Imperialism* (New Haven, CT: Yale University Press, 2007), 11.
7. Caner and Caner, *Unveiling Islam*, 40.
8. Ibid., 46.
9. Karsh, *Islamic Imperialism*, 13.
10. Caner and Caner, *Unveiling Islam*, 46.
11. Karsh, *Islamic Imperialism*, 15.
12. Ibid.
13. Ibid., 17.
14. Ibid., 222.
15. Ibid., 231.
16. Bernard Lewis, *What Went Wrong? The Clash Between Islam and Modernity in the Middle East* (New York: Harper Perennial, 2002), 4.
17. Christopher Caldwell, *Reflections on the Revolution in Europe: Immigration, Islam and the West* (New York, NY: Doubleday, 2009), 11–19.

18. Mu'ammar al-Qadhafi, *Middle East Media Research Institute,* "Special Dispatch #1152," Al-Jazeera, April 10, 2006.
19. Lewis, *What Went Wrong?,* 4.
20. Caner and Caner, *Unveiling Islam,* 72.
21. Lewis, *What Went Wrong?,* 6.
22. Caner and Caner, *Unveiling Islam,* 74.
23. Karen Armstrong, "Islam's Awakening," *U.S. News and World Report,* Special Edition 2009, 62.
24. Paul Johnson, *Churchill* (New York: Viking, 2009), 60.
25. Ibid.
26. Ibid., 61.
27. Ibid., 63.
28. Shimon Apisdorf, *Judaism in a Nutshell: Israel* (Rochester, NY: Leviathan Press, 2002), 67.
29. Ibid.
30. Ibid., 70.
31. The Pew Forum, "Mapping the Global Muslim Population," October 8, 2009, http://pewresearch.org/pubs/1370/mapping-size-distribution-worlds-muslim-population (accessed February 17, 2010).

Chapter 11: The Christian Perspective

1. Daniel Schwammenthal, "The Forgotten Palestinian Refugees," *Wall Street Journal,* December 28, 2009, http://online.wsj.com/article/SB10001424052748704304504574610022765965390.html (accessed January 18, 2010).

Some Final Thoughts: Three Burning Questions

1. Attributed to Jim Deloach.

Glossary

1. *Encyclopedia.com,* s.v. "Arafat, Yasser" (by *The Columbia Encyclopedia,* 6th ed.), http://www.encyclopedia.com (accessed February 15, 2010).
2. Trent C. Butler, *Holman Bible Dictionary,* s.v. "Assyria, History and Religion of," http://www.studylight.org/dic/hbd/view.cgi?number=T539 (accessed February 10, 2010).
3. Ibid., s.v. "David," http://www.studylight.org/dic/hbd/view.cgi?number=T1527 (accessed February 10, 2010).
4. *Dictionary.com,* s.v. "Gulf of Aqaba" (by *The American Heritage Dictionary of the English Language,* 4th ed.), http://dictionary.reference.com/browse/gulf of aqaba (accessed February 17, 2010).

5. Ibid., s.v. "Havilah" (by *Easton's 1897 Bible Dictionary*), http://dictionary.reference.com/browse/havilah (accessed February 15, 2010).

6. Butler, *Holman Bible Dictionary*, s.v. "Hebron," http://www.studylight.org/dic/hbd/view.cgi?number=T2668 (accessed February 10, 2010).

7. Ibid., s.v. "Herod," http://www.studylight.org/dic/hbd/view.cgi?number=T2741 (accessed February 10, 2010).

8. *Dictionary.com*, s.v. "Herzl" (by *The American Heritage Dictionary of the English Language*, 4th ed.), http://dictionary.reference.com/browse/herzl (accessed February 10, 2010).

9. Butler, *Holman Bible Dictionary*, s.v. "Hittites and Hevites," http://www.studylight.org/dic/hbd/view.cgi?number=T2796 (accessed February 10, 2010).

10. Ibid., s.v. "Jacob," http://www.studylight.org/dic/hbd/view.cgi?number=T3186 (accessed February 10, 2010).

11. The Jewish Virtual Library, "Jerusalem—The Old City," http://www.jewishvirtuallibrary.org/jsource/vie/Jerusalem2.html#Jewish (accessed February 25, 2010).

12. *Dictionary.com*, s.v. "Jordan" (by *The American Heritage Dictionary of the English Language*, 4th ed.), http://dictionary.reference.com/browse/jordan (accessed February 15, 2010).

13. Butler, *Holman Bible Dictionary*, s.v. "Joseph," http://www.studylight.org/dic/hbd/view.cgi?number=T3493 (accessed February 10, 2010).

14. *Dictionary.com*, s.v. "Judaism" (by *The American Heritage Dictionary of the English Language*, 4th ed.), http://dictionary.reference.com/browse/judaism (accessed February 10, 2010).

15. Butler, *Holman Bible Dictionary*, s.v. "Kadesh-barnea," http://www.studylight.org/dic/hbd/view.cgi?number=T3555 (accessed February 10, 2010).

16. *Dictionary.com*, s.v. "Kahn, Genghis" (by *The American Heritage New Dictionary of Cultural Literacy*, 3rd ed.), http://dictionary.reference.com/browse/genghis khan (accessed February 10, 2010).

17. *Encyclopedia.com*, s.v. "Khomeini, Ayatollah Ruhollah" (by *The Columbia Encyclopedia*, 6th ed.), http://www.encyclopedia.com/topic/Ayatollah_Ruhollah_Khomeini.aspx (accessed February 15, 2010).

18. Butler, *Holman Bible Dictionary*, s.v. "Laban," http://www.studylight.org/dic/hbd/view.cgi?number=T3723 (accessed February 10, 2010).

19. *Dictionary.com*, s.v. "Mao tse-Tung" (by *The American Heritage New Dictionary of Cultural Literacy*, 3rd ed.), http://dictionary.reference.com/browse/mao tse-tung (accessed February 10, 2010).

20. Ibid., s.v. "Marxism" (by *The American Heritage New Dictionary of Cultural Literacy*, 3rd ed.), http://dictionary.reference.com/browse/marxism (accessed February 10, 2010).

21. Ibid., s.v. "Mecca" (by *The American Heritage Dictionary of the English Language*, 4th ed.), http://dictionary.reference.com/browse/mecca (accessed February 10, 2010).

22. Ibid., s.v. "Medina" (by *The American Heritage Dictionary of the English Language*, 4th ed.), http://dictionary.reference.com/browse/medina (accessed February 10, 2010).

23. *Encyclopedia.com*, s.v. "Middle East" (by *The Columbia Encyclopedia*, 6th ed.), http://www.encyclopedia.com/topic/Middle_East.aspx (accessed February 15, 2010).

24. Butler, *Holman Bible Dictionary*, s.v. "Mordecai," http://www.studylight.org/dic/hbd/view.cgi?number=T4394 (accessed February 10, 2010).

25. Ibid., s.v. "Moses," http://www.studylight.org/dic/hbd/view.cgi?number=T4404 (accessed February 10, 2010).

26. *Dictionary.com*, s.v. "Nasser" (by *The American Heritage Dictionary of the English Language*, 4th ed.), http://dictionary.reference.com/browse/nasser (accessed February 10, 2010).

27. Ibid., s.v. "Nazism" (by *The American Heritage Dictionary of the English Language*, 4th ed.), http://dictionary.reference.com/browse/nazism (accessed February 10, 2010).

28. Ibid., s.v. "Ottoman empire" (by *The American Heritage New Dictionary of Cultural Literacy*, 3rd ed.), http://dictionary.reference.com/browse/ottoman empire (accessed February 10, 2010).

29. Butler, *Holman Bible Dictionary*, s.v. "Paddan-aram," http://www.studylight.org/dic/hbd/view.cgi?number=T4775 (accessed February 10, 2010).

30. Ibid., s.v. "Paul," http://www.studylight.org/dic/hbd/view.cgi?number=T4860 (accessed February 10, 2010).

31. *Dictionary.com*, s.v. "Persian Gulf War" (by *The American Heritage New Dictionary of Cultural Literacy*, 3rd ed.), http://dictionary.reference.com/browse/persian gulf war (accessed February 10, 2010).

32. Butler, *Holman Bible Dictionary*, s.v. "Pilate, Pontius," http://www.studylight.org/dic/hbd/view.cgi?number=T4991 (accessed February 10, 2010).

33. *Dictionary.com*, s.v. "Qaddafi" (by *The American Heritage Dictionary of the English Language*, 4th ed.), http://dictionary.reference.com/browse/qaddafi (accessed February 10, 2010).

34. Ibid., s.v. "Saudi Arabia" (by *The American Heritage New Dictionary of Cultural Literacy*, 3rd ed.), http://dictionary.reference.com/browse/saudi arabia (accessed February 10, 2010).

35. Ibid., s.v. "Shiites" (by *The American Heritage Dictionary of the English Language*, 4th ed.), http://dictionary.reference.com/browse/shiites (accessed February 10, 2010).

36. Butler, *Holman Bible Dictionary*, s.v. "Shur, Wilderness of," http://www

.studylight.org/dic/hbd/view.cgi?number=T5868 (accessed February 10, 2010).

37. *Dictionary.com*, s.v. "Sinai" (by *The American Heritage New Dictionary of Cultural Literacy*, 3rd ed.), http://dictionary.reference.com/browse/sinai (accessed February 10, 2010).

38. Ibid., s.v. "Stalin" (by *The American Heritage Dictionary of the English Language*, 4th ed.), http://dictionary.reference.com/browse/stalin (accessed February 10, 2010).

39. Ibid., s.v. "Sunni" (by *The American Heritage Dictionary of the English Language*, 4th ed.), http://dictionary.reference.com/browse/sunni (accessed February 11, 2010).

40. Ibid., s.v. "Syria" (by *The American Heritage Dictionary of the English Language*, 4th ed.), http://dictionary.reference.com/browse/syria (accessed February 11, 2010).

41. *Sacred Destinations.com*, s.v. "Temple Mount, Jerusalem," http://www .sacred-destinations.com/israel/jerusalem-temple-mount (accessed February 19, 2010).

42. Butler, *Holman Bible Dictionary*, s.v. "Euphrates and Tigris Rivers," http:// www.studylight.org/dic/hbd/view.cgi?number=T1958 (accessed February 10, 2010).

43. *Dictionary.com*, s.v. "Transjordan" (by *Random House Unabridged Dictionary*), http://dictionary.reference.com/browse/transjordan (accessed February 10, 2010).

44. Ibid., s.v. "West Bank" (by *The American Heritage Dictionary of the English Language*, 4th ed.), http://dictionary.reference.com/browse/west bank (accessed February 11, 2010).

45. Ibid., s.v. "Zionism" (by *The American Heritage New Dictionary of Cultural Literacy*, 3rd ed.), http://dictionary.reference.com/browse/zionism (accessed February 10, 2010).

About the Author

B ryant Wright is the only pastor the seventy-five-hundred–
member Johnson Ferry Baptist Church of Marietta, Georgia, has
ever had. He is also the founder of Right from the Heart media
ministry, which airs one-minute and also thirty-second inspirational
spots, broadcast in four languages and heard in six countries—mostly
on secular radio and television. In addition, Right from the Heart offers
a teaching ministry and daily devotionals on the Internet. Wright gradu-
ated from the University of South Carolina and holds a master of divinity
from Southern Baptist Theological Seminary and an honorary doctorate
from SEFOVAN Seminary in Madrid, Spain. He and his wife are the parents of three grown sons.

www.rightfromtheheart.org